English in Focus: Electrical Engineering and Electronics

ENGLISH IN FOCUS

English in Electrical Engineering and Electronics

ERIC H. GLENDINNING

OXFORD UNIVERSITY PRESS

Oxford University Press, Walton Street, Oxford OX2 6DP

OXFORD NEW YORK TORONTO
PETALING JAYA SINGAPORE HONG KONG TOKYO
DELHI BOMBAY CALCUTTA MADRAS KARACHI
NAIROBI DAR ES SALAAM CAPE TOWN
MELBOURNE AUCKLAND

and associated companies in
BERLIN IBADAN

OXFORD is a trade mark of Oxford University Press

ISBN 0 19 437517 X (Student's Book)
ISBN 0 19 437508 0 (Teacher's Edition)

First published 1980
Tenth impression 1988

Printed in Hungary

Contents

Unit 2

Unit 3

Introduction

The aim of this book is to develop a basic knowledge of how English is used for communication in electrical engineering and electronics. It is intended for students who already know how to handle the common English sentence patterns but who need to learn how these patterns are used in scientific and technical writing to convey information and to develop logical arguments.

The exercises direct the student's attention to certain features of English which are specific to scientific and technical writing. The aim is to provide the student with a strategy for reading more difficult electrical engineering and electronics texts and to prepare him for making effective use of English in his own writing.

Although the emphasis is on English as a medium of expression in electrical engineering and electronics, the basic elements of the language have not been neglected. Pattern practice is provided, particularly in the Use of Language and Guided Writing sections of each unit, but this kind of work is always presented in relation to a scientific context and not simply as an exercise in making sentences for their own sake.

This book does not aim at teaching the subject-matter of electrical engineering and electronics, and it does not aim at teaching grammatical structures and vocabulary as such. Its purpose is to show how language is used as a medium for the study of electrical engineering and electronics, and so to give students a grounding in one particular set of communication skills in English.

Acknowledgements

My grateful thanks are due to several people for the successful completion of this book: to my wife for her patience, to my brother, Mr Norman Glendinning, for his advice on the technical content and the care with which he prepared many of the illustrations, to Mr Roy M. Tatton B.Sc., M.Sc., for checking the accuracy of the technical content, and to those students of Edinburgh Language Foundation with whom successive drafts were tested.

The publishers would like to thank the undermentioned for permission to reproduce the following diagrams:

Chapman and Hall, Table 3 page 61, from *Microwaves, Communication and Radar*, Solymar, L., 1974.
Electricity Council, Table 4 page 61, from Industrial Data Sheet 44.
Engineering Industries Training Board, Oscilloscope page 18, from Module J22; Frequency changing transducer page 67, from Module J24.
Mawdsley's Limited, Cutaway diagram of dc motor page 27.
Mullard Limited, Circuit page 23; Transistor characteristics page 90, from *Mullard Silicon Power Transistor Range*, chart 5501/3m/572.
Newnes-Butterworth, moving-coil meter page 47, from *Electronics, A Course Book for Students*, Olsen, G. H., 1973; Table 3 page 61, from *Newnes Electrical Pocket Book*, Reeves, E. A., 1975.

Unit 1

I READING AND COMPREHENSION

CONDUCTORS, INSULATORS AND SEMICONDUCTORS

If we connect a battery across a body, there is a movement of free electrons towards the positive end. This movement of electrons is an electric current. All materials can be classified into three groups according to how readily they permit an electric current to flow. These are: conductors, insulators and semiconductors.

In the first category are substances which provide an easy path for an electric current. All metals are conductors, however some metals do not conduct well. Manganin, for example, is a poor conductor. Copper is a good conductor, therefore it is widely used for cables. A non-metal which conducts well is carbon. Salt water is an example of a liquid conductor.

A material which does not easily release electrons is called an insulator. Rubber, nylon, porcelain and air are all insulators. There are no perfect insulators. All insulators will allow some flow of electrons, however this can usually be ignored because the flow they permit is so small.

Semiconductors are midway between conductors and insulators. Under certain conditions they allow a current to flow easily but under others they behave as insulators. Germanium and silicon are semiconductors. Mixtures of certain metallic oxides also act as semiconductors. These are known as thermistors. The resistance of thermistors falls rapidly as their temperature rises. They are therefore used in temperature-sensing devices.

EXERCISE A *Rephrasing*

Rewrite the following sentences, replacing the words in italics with expressions from the passage which have similar meanings:

1. The *flow* of free electrons is an electric current.
2. Materials in the first *group* are called conductors.
3. *Materials* which provide a path for an electric current are conductors.
4. All insulators *permit* some flow of electrons.
5. Germanium sometimes *acts* as an insulator and sometimes as a conductor.

EXERCISE B *Contextual reference*

What do the pronouns in italics in these sentences refer to?

1. All materials can be classified into three groups according to how readily *they* permit an electric current to flow. (line 3)
   (a) three groups
   (b) all materials
   (c) free electrons

2. Under certain conditions *they* allow a current to flow easily but under others they behave as insulators. (line 16)
   (a) conductors
   (b) semiconductors
   (c) insulators

3. *These* are known as thermistors. (line 18)
   (a) metallic oxides
   (b) semiconductors
   (c) mixtures of certain metallic oxides

4. *They* are therefore used in temperature-sensing devices. (line 20)
   (a) thermistors
   (b) semiconductors
   (c) metallic oxides

EXERCISE C *Checking facts and ideas*

Decide if these statements are true or false. Quote from the passage to support your decisions.

1. Electrons flow from positive to negative.
2. Copper provides an easy path for an electric current.
3. All metals are good conductors.
4. All good conductors are metals.
5. Air is not a perfect insulator.
6. Rubber readily releases electrons.
7. The resistance of a thermistor is higher at low temperatures than at high temperatures.

II USE OF LANGUAGE

EXERCISE D *Describing shapes*

Study these nouns and adjectives for describing the shapes of objects:

shape	noun	adjective	shape	noun	adjective
2 dimensional			3 dimensional		
	circle	circular		sphere	spherical
	semi-circle	semi-circular		cylinder	cylindrical
	square	square		tube	tubular
	rectangle	rectangular		—	rectangular
lines			edges		
		straight			rounded
		curved			pointed

When something has a regular geometric shape we can use one of the adjectives from the table to describe it.

EXAMPLE

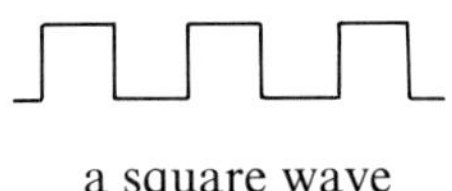

a square wave

When the object has no recognized geometric shape but does resemble a well-known object or a letter of the alphabet, it may be described in one of the following ways:

EXAMPLES

an H-shaped antenna   a saw-tooth wave

Now describe the shapes of the following objects as completely as possible:

1. a ceramic capacitor
2. transformer laminations

3. an electrolytic capacitor

4. an antenna

5. a magnet

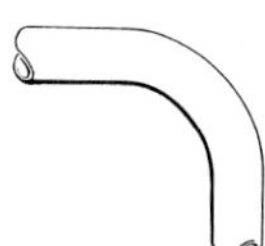

6. a cable conduit

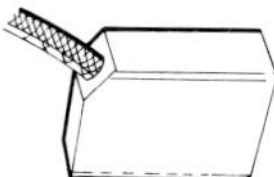

7. a carbon brush

8. a capacitor

9. a motor pole shoe

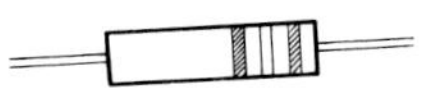

10. a resistor

EXERCISE E *Describing position and connection*

When describing the position of a component or how it is connected in a circuit, phrases of this pattern are used:

be + past participle + preposition

EXAMPLES

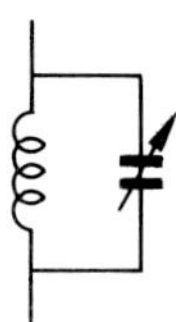

1. The tuning capacitor IS CONNECTED ACROSS the coil.

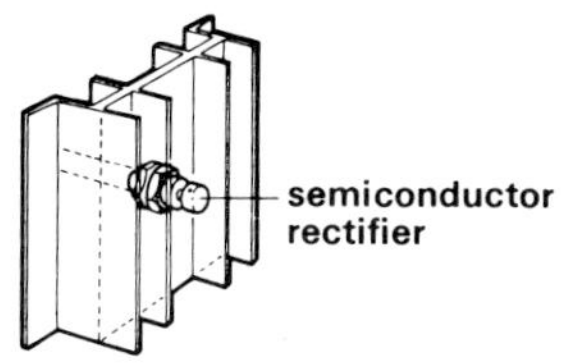

2. The semiconductor rectifier IS MOUNTED ON the heat sink.

Now complete each sentence using an appropriate phrase from this list:

wound round	located within
connected across	applied to
mounted on	connected to
wired to	connected between

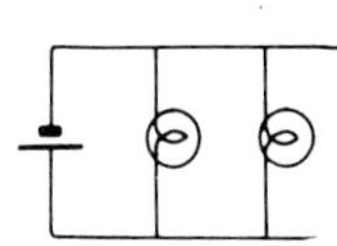

1. the lamps are ...... the battery.

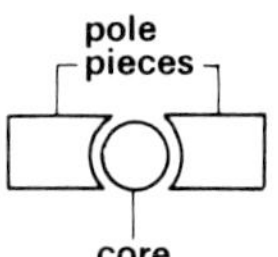

2. The core is ..... the pole pieces.

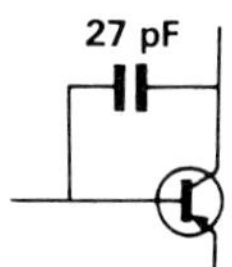

3. The 27pF capacitor is ...... the collector and the base.

4. The antenna is ...... the coil.

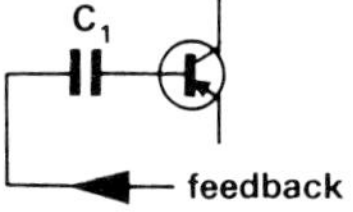

5. Feedback voltage is ...... the base of the transistor through C_1.

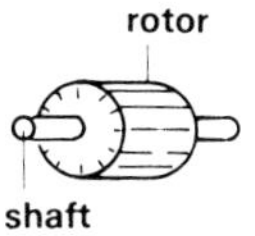

6. The rotor is ...... the shaft.

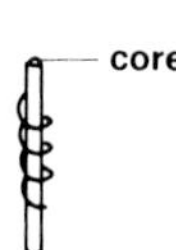

7. The coil is . . . . . . an iron core.

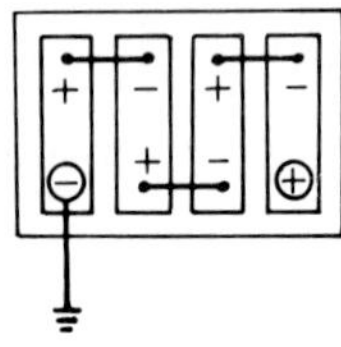

8. The negative pole of the battery . . . . . . earth.

EXERCISE F *Writing instructions 1*

Simple instructions use the infinitive.

EXAMPLES

1. Measure the collector current.
2. Switch off the supply.
3. Do not solder transistors without a heat-shunt.

Study these instructions for an experiment to measure the total resistance of resistors in series using the circuit in Figure 1.

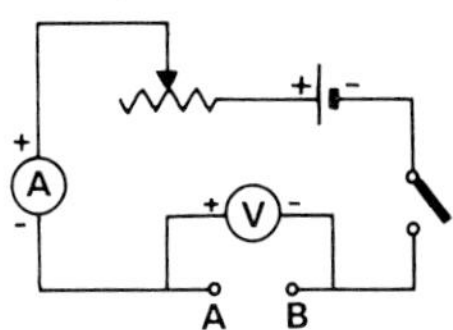

FIGURE 1

1. Use a high-resistance voltmeter and a low-resistance ammeter.
2. Connect R_1 across AB.
3. Close the switch and adjust the rheostat until both meters show almost full scale deflection.
4. Take simultaneous readings of both voltage and current.
5. Calculate R_1 by the formula $R = \frac{V}{I}$.
6. Repeat this for R_2.
7. Connect R_1 and R_2 in series across AB.
8. Calculate the total resistance using the same formula as before.
9. Tabulate the results.

Now write your own instructions for an experiment to measure the total resistance of resistors in parallel, using the same circuit. Begin like this:

1. Connect up the apparatus as shown in Figure 1.

EXERCISE G *Describing an experiment*

Make a description of the first experiment in Exercise F by rewriting each instruction in the present passive.

EXAMPLE

1. Use a high-resistance voltmeter and a low-resistance ammeter.
   A HIGH-RESISTANCE VOLTMETER AND A LOW-RESISTANCE AMMETER ARE USED.

EXERCISE H *Reporting an experiment*

Make a report of the second experiment in Exercise F by rewriting each of your instructions in the past passive.

EXAMPLE

1. Connect up the apparatus as shown in Figure 1.
   THE APPARATUS WAS CONNECTED UP as shown in Figure 1.

EXERCISE I *Writing instructions 2*

Study this description of how batteries are charged:

> The filler plugs are removed and the battery is connected to the charger. It must be ensured that the correct polarity is observed and good connections are made. The charger is then switched on. The charger is switched off when the battery has been fully charged. The specific gravity of a sample cell is checked. The filler plugs are replaced and the battery left to cool before use.

Now begin a list of instructions for how to charge a battery. Begin like this:

1. Remove the filler plugs.

EXERCISE J *Relative clauses 1*

Study these sentences:

1. Starter motor brushes are made of carbon.
2. The carbon contains copper.

Both these sentences refer to carbon. We can link them by making sentence 2 a relative clause.

1+2. Starter motor brushes are made of carbon WHICH CONTAINS COPPER.

The *relative clause* is in capitals. Note that THE CARBON in sentence 2 becomes WHICH.

Study these other pairs of sentences and note how they are linked:

3. Industrial consumers are supplied at higher voltages than domestic consumers.
4. These consumers use large quantities of energy.

3+4. Consumers WHO USE LARGE QUANTITIES OF ENERGY are supplied at higher voltages than domestic consumers.

5. 33kV lines are fed to intermediate substations.
6. In the intermediate substations the voltage is stepped down to 11kV.

5+6. 33kV lines are fed to intermediate substations WHERE THE VOLTAGE IS STEPPED DOWN TO 11kV.

Now link these sentences. Make the second sentence in each pair a relative clause:

1. The coil is connected in series with a resistor.
   The resistor has a value of 240 ohms.
2. The supply is fed to a distribution substation.
   The supply is reduced to 415 V in the distribution substation.
3. Workers require a high degree of illumination.
   The workers assemble very small precision instruments.
4. Manganin is a metal.
   This metal has a comparatively high resistance.
5. The signal passes to the detector.
   The signal is rectified by the detector.
6. A milliammeter is an instrument.
   The instrument is used for measuring small currents.
7. Workers require illumination of 300 lux.
   The workers assemble heavy machinery.
8. Armoured cables are used in places.
   There is a risk of mechanical damage in these places.

EXERCISE K *Reason and result connectives 1*

Study these sentences:

1. Copper is used for cables.
2. Copper is a good conductor.

Sentence 1 tells us what copper is used for. Sentence 2 tells us why it is used. Sentence 2 provides a reason for sentence 1. We can link a statement and a reason using *because*.

1+2. Copper is used for cables BECAUSE it is a good conductor.

When the reason is a noun or a noun phrase, we use *because of*.

EXAMPLE

The motor overheated BECAUSE OF dirt in the air gap.

Now study this pair:

3. The flow of electrons through an insulator is very small.
4. The flow can be ignored.

Sentence 4 is the result of sentence 3. We can link a statement and a result using *therefore*.

3+4. The flow of electrons through an insulator is very small, THEREFORE it can be ignored.

Note that a comma is used before *therefore*.

Now link these ideas using *because* or *therefore*.

1. Soft iron is used in electromagnets.
   Soft iron can be magnetized easily.
2. The voltage is 250 V and the current 5 A.
   The resistance is 50 Ω.
3. Pvc is used to cover cables.
   Pvc is a good insulator.
4. Transistors can be damaged by heat.
   Care must be taken when soldering transistors.
5. Capacitance is usually measured in microfarads or picofarads.
   The farad is too large a unit.
6. Output transistors are mounted on a heat sink.
   Output transistors generate heat.
7. It is easy to control the speed of dc motors.
   Dc motors are used when variable speeds are required.
8. A cathode-ray tube screen glows when an electron beam strikes it.
   The screen is coated with a phosphor.

EXERCISE L *Pronoun links between sentences*

When we link sentences together, or into paragraphs, repeated nouns usually become pronouns.

EXAMPLES

1. A short circuit occurs in a transformer.
2. The short circuit may cause overheating.
3. The overheating may further damage the insulation.

When a short circuit occurs in a transformer, IT may cause overheating. THIS may further damage the insulation.

When there may be misunderstanding, or when the repeated noun comes a long time after its first mention, the full noun is used.

EXAMPLE

First the pole shoes and coils are drawn out of the yoke. Then the coils are removed from them and new coils are fitted over them. Next they are refitted inside the yoke and located by lightly tightening the fixing screws. Finally they are tightened fully and their terminals are soldered.

Compare this version where the full nouns have been kept:

> First the pole shoes and coils are drawn out of the yoke. Then the coils are removed from the shoes and new coils fitted over the shoes. Next the shoes are refitted inside the yoke and located by lightly tightening the fixing screws. Finally the screws are tightened fully and the new coil terminals are soldered.

Now replace the repeated nouns in this paragraph with suitable pronouns where there is no likelihood of confusion.

> A transformer is a device which changes the magnitude of an ac voltage. The transformer consists of a primary coil to which the input is applied, and a secondary coil from which the output is obtained. The coils are insulated and wound round a former. The coils have a core of soft iron on which the former is mounted. The core is made from many thin sheets or laminations. The sheets are oxidized so that the sheets are insulated from each other. Oxidizing the sheets reduces eddy losses.

III INFORMATION TRANSFER

EXERCISE M *Mathematical symbols used in electrical engineering and electronics*

Study the table of mathematical symbols used in electrical engineering and electronics in Appendix 1. Then write out the following expressions in full.

EXAMPLE

$$I = \frac{V}{R}$$

I *is equal to* V *over* R.

1. $P = I^2 \times R$
2. $\frac{1}{R_{tot}} = \frac{1}{R_1} + \frac{1}{R_2} + \frac{1}{R_3}$
3. $B \propto H$
4. $X_L = \sqrt{Z^2 - R^2}$
5. $V = IR$
6. Frequency stability $\approx$ 0·04%/°C
7. $\frac{\text{output frequency}}{\text{input frequency}} \approx 10:1$
8. $Z = \frac{100 \times 10^4}{200 \times 10^{-5}}$
9. collector dissipation $\triangleq$ 12 milliwatts
10. tolerance $\pm$ 5%

IV GUIDED WRITING

STAGE 1 *Sentence building*

Join the following groups of sentences to make ten longer sentences. Use the words printed in italics at the beginning of each group. You may omit words and make whatever changes you think are necessary in the word order and punctuation of the sentences.

1. *or*
   Circuits can be protected from excessive currents by a fuse.
   Circuits can be protected from excessive currents by a circuit breaker.
2. *however*
   A fuse is the simplest and cheapest protection.
   For accurate and repetitive operation a circuit breaker is used.
3. *which*
   A simple circuit breaker consists of a solenoid and a switch with contacts.
   The contacts are held closed by a latch.
4. *thus energizing*
   The current from the supply line flows through the switch and solenoid coil.
   This energizes the solenoid.
5. *which, therefore*
   At normal currents the pull of the solenoid on the latch will not overcome the tension of the spring.
   The spring holds the latch in place.
   The switch remains closed.
6. *if*
   The current rises to a dangerous level.
   The pull of the solenoid on the latch increases.
7. *and*
   The increased pull overcomes the latch spring tension.
   The increased pull pulls the latch towards the solenoid.
8. *which*
   This releases the switch contacts.
   The switch contacts are pulled apart by a spring.
9. *as*
   The circuit is now broken.
   The unit is protected.
10. *when*
    The fault in the supply or unit is put right.
    The latch can be reset.

STAGE 2 *Diagram labelling*

Label this diagram with the following:
solenoid, latch, switch contacts, latch spring, switch spring

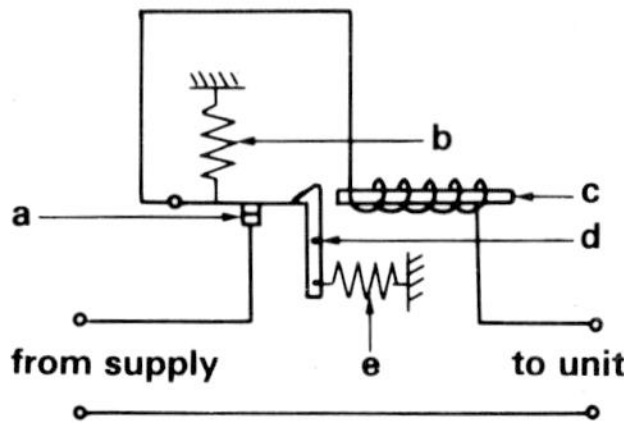

STAGE 3 *Paragraph building*

Group your completed sentences into two paragraphs. Label the diagram Figure 1 and insert a reference to it in the completed passage.

EXAMPLES

See Figure 1. Study Figure 1.

Finally give the passage a suitable title.

V READING AND SUMMARIZING

STAGE 1 *Comprehension*

Study this passage carefully and answer the questions which follow:

SUPERCONDUCTIVITY

The resistance of metals varies with their temperature. When they get hot, their resistance increases. When they cool, their resistance falls. The resistance of some metals and alloys steadily decreases as their temperature is lowered, then falls suddenly to a negligible value at temperatures a few degrees above absolute zero ($-273°C$). In other words, these materials have almost no resistance to an electric current at very low temperatures. They become almost perfect conductors. This is called superconductivity. It occurs only with certain materials, for example lead, and only at very low temperatures.

The practical applications of superconductivity are limited because of the very low temperatures required. A number of uses, however, have been proposed. If a current is induced by a magnetic field in a ring of superconducting material, it will continue to circulate when the magnetic field is removed. In theory this could be made use of in the memory cells of computers. Memory cells made of superconducting materials could store information indefinitely. Because of the zero resistivity of the cells, the information could be retrieved very quickly, as fast as 10^{-8} seconds.

A high percentage of the total losses in modern transformers is due to the resistance of the windings. Transformers could be made with windings cooled to the low temperatures at which superconductivity occurs. The resistance of the windings would be zero and the transformer would be almost ideal. Similarly a 100% efficient electric motor has been proposed using the magnetic field of superconducting coils.

1. Name a superconducting material.
2. When do materials exhibit superconductivity?
3. Why are the practical applications limited?
4. What applications have been proposed?
5. What advantages would a memory cell made of a superconducting material have?
6. How efficient would transformers and motors be which used superconductivity?

STAGE 2 *Summarizing*

Complete this summary of the passage using your answers to Stage 1:

Some materials, for example . . . . . ., become almost perfect conductors at . . . . . .
The applications of superconductivity are limited because . . . . . .
Possible uses are . . . . . .
A superconducting memory cell would allow information . . . . . .
A transformer or motor using superconductivity would be . . . . . .

Unit 2

I READING AND COMPREHENSION

CIRCUIT ELEMENTS

Current moves from a point of high potential energy to one of low potential. It can only do so if there is a path for it to follow. This path is called an electric circuit. All circuits contain four elements: a source, a load, a transmission system and a control.

The source provides the electromotive force. This establishes the difference in potential which makes current flow possible. The source can be any device which supplies electrical energy. For example, it may be a generator or a battery.

The load converts the electrical energy from the source into some other form of energy. For instance, a lamp changes electrical energy into light and heat. The load can be any electrical device.

The transmission system conducts the current round the circuit. Any conductor can be part of a transmission system. Most systems consist of wires. It is often possible, however, for the metal frame of a unit to be one section of its transmission system. For example, the metal chassis of many electrical devices are used to conduct current. Similarly the body of a car is part of its electrical transmission system.

The control regulates the current flow in the circuit. It may control the current by limiting it, as does a rheostat, or by interrupting it, as does a switch.

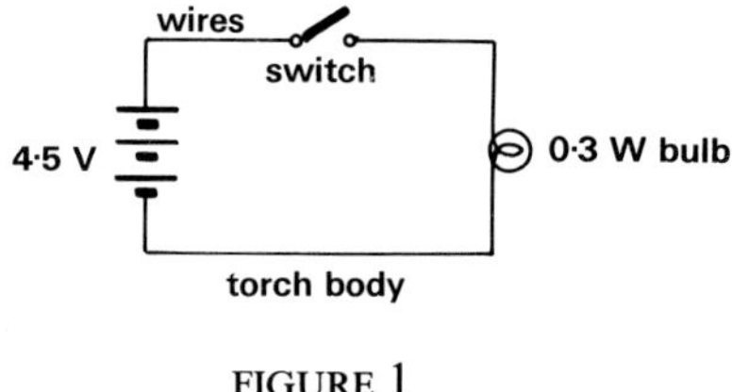

FIGURE 1

Study Figure 1. In this simple flashlight circuit, the source comprises three 1·5 V cells in series. The load is a 0·3 W bulb. Part of the transmission system is the metal body of the flashlight, and the control is a sliding switch.

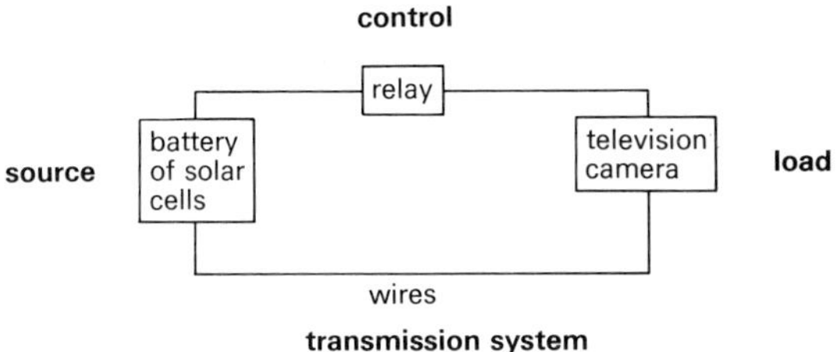

FIGURE 2

Compare Figure 2. The function of this circuit is to operate a television camera aboard a space satellite. Here the source is a battery of solar cells. A solar cell is an electric cell which converts sunlight into electrical energy. The load is the television camera. The transmission system is the connecting wires. The control is a relay actuated by transmissions from ground control. Although the function of this circuit is much more complex than that of the flashlight, it too consists of the four basic elements.

EXERCISE A *Rephrasing*

Rewrite the following sentences, replacing the words in italics with expressions from the passage which have a similar meaning.

1. A lamp *converts* electrical energy into light.
2. The generator *provides* the circuit with electromotive force.
3. The metal *frame* of the oscilloscope is part of its transmission system.
4. The rheostat *controls* the current flow in the circuit.
5. A battery of solar cells *supplies* power to the circuit.

EXERCISE B *Contextual reference*

What do the pronouns in italics in these sentences refer to?

1. Current moves from a point of high potential energy to *one* of low potential. (line 1)
   (a) current
   (b) energy
   (c) a point
2. For example, *it* may be a generator or a battery. (line 7)
   (a) the source
   (b) a device
   (c) electromotive force
3. It is often possible, however, for the metal frame of a unit to be one section of *its* transmission system. (line 13)
   (a) the metal frame's
   (b) the unit's
   (c) the circuit's

4. Although the function of this circuit is much more complex than that of the flashlight, *it* too consists of the four basic elements. (line 27)
(a) this circuit
(b) the function
(c) the flashlight

EXERCISE C *Checking facts and ideas*

Decide if these statements are true or false. Quote from the passage to support your decisions.

1. A difference in potential is required before current can flow in a circuit.
2. A generator is a source of electromotive force.
3. Loads convert electrical energy into light and heat.
4. Transmission systems must consist of wires.
5. A rheostat may be used as a control.
6. The load in the flashlight circuit is a bulb.
7. The source in the satellite circuit is a solar cell.
8. The current flow in the satellite circuit is regulated by a relay.
9. The flashlight circuit differs basically from the satellite circuit.

II USE OF LANGUAGE

EXERCISE D *Describing function*

When we answer the question *What does X do?*, we describe the function of X.

EXAMPLE

What does a fuse do? It protects a circuit.

We can emphasize function by using this pattern:

The function of a fuse is to protect a circuit.

Now identify these components using Appendix 3 if necessary. Explain the function of each component with the help of this list.

(a) adds capacitance to a circuit
(b) rectifies alternating currents
(c) adds resistance to a circuit
(d) measures very small currents
(e) breaks a circuit
(f) protects a circuit
(g) varies the current in a circuit

(h) transforms ac voltages
(i) receives rf signals
(j) selects a frequency

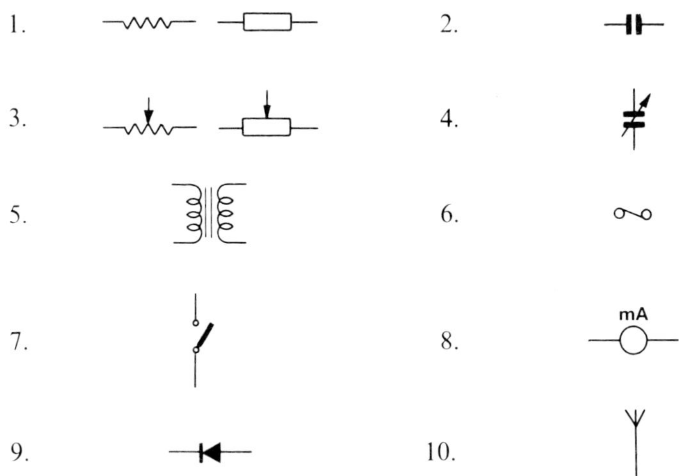

EXERCISE E *Describing purpose*

When we answer the question *What is X for?*, we describe the purpose of X.

EXAMPLE

What is an ammeter for? It is for measuring current.

Other ways we can describe the purpose of an ammeter are:

1. It is used for measuring current.
2. It is used to measure current.
3. We measure current with an ammeter.
4. We measure current using an ammeter.

Now describe the purpose of these instruments and tools using any of the structures presented above.

1. a voltmeter
2. a soldering iron
3. a milliammeter
4. an oscilloscope
5. a heat sink
6. wire-clippers
7. a megger
8. an ohmmeter
9. a signal generator
10. a battery charger

EXERCISE F *Describing means*

Study this diagram. It shows the controls of an oscilloscope. Some of them have been numbered.

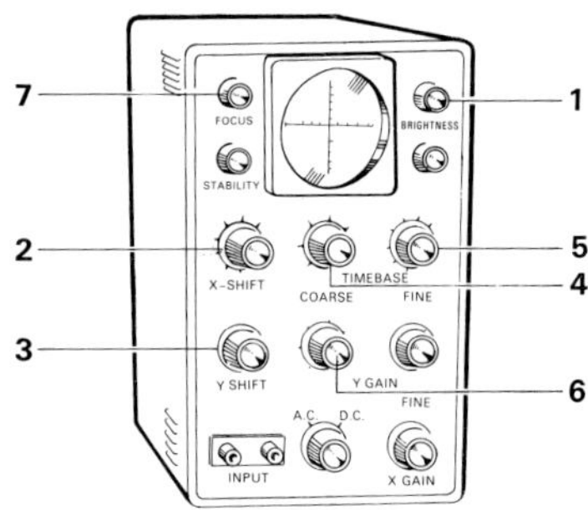

Study this information about the focus control:

	Control	Function	Means
7	FOCUS	Focuses the electron lens.	Varies the potential on $anode_2$.

Using this information, we can answer three questions:

1. What does the focus control do?
2. What is the focus control for?
3. How does the focus control work?

Question 1 is about function. As you have seen, we can answer it like this:

The focus control focuses the electron lens.

Question 2 is about purpose. We can answer it like this:

The focus control is for focusing the electron lens.

Question 3 is about means. It asks for an explanation of how the focus control works. We can answer it in this way:

The focus control focuses the electron lens by varying the potential on $anode_2$.

Or we can say:

The focus control varies the potential on $anode_2$, thereby focusing the electron lens.

Now ask and answer questions about the function, purpose and means of operation of the controls listed in this table.

	Control	Function	Means
1	BRIGHTNESS	Varies the intensity of the beam.	Varies the negative potential on the grid.
2	X SHIFT	Moves the trace along the X axis.	Alters the biasing of the X amplifier.
3	Y SHIFT	Moves the trace along the Y axis.	Alters the biasing of the Y amplifier.
4	COARSE FREQUENCY	Selects the approximate time base frequency.	Selects a capacitor in the timebase oscillator.
5	FINE FREQUENCY	Adjusts the timebase frequency.	Varies a resistor in the timebase oscillator.
6	Y GAIN	Controls the signal amplification.	Alters the gain of the Y amplifier.

EXERCISE G *Explaining controls*

Explain the controls of any other piece of equipment you are familiar with, e.g. a multimeter, a transmitter, a receiver.

EXERCISE H *Relative clauses 2: making definitions*

Study these two sentences:

The cables were undamaged.
The cables were armoured.

We can link them in two ways using a relative clause:

1. The cables WHICH WERE ARMOURED were undamaged.
2. The cables, WHICH WERE ARMOURED, were undamaged.

Sentence 1 means that only the armoured cables were undamaged. Other cables, for example pvc coated cables, were damaged. The relative clause is a defining one. It defines the type of cable which was undamaged. It carries essential information.

Sentence 2 means that all the cables were undamaged and all the cables were armoured. The relative clause is a non-defining one. It adds some extra information to the sentence but it is not essential. We can remove it from the sentence and the sentence still makes good sense. It is separated from the rest of the sentence by commas.

One use of defining relative clauses is to make definitions. Study this diagram:

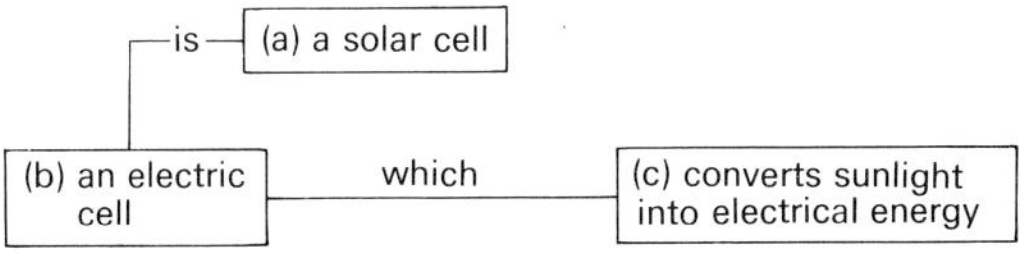

We can make a definition of a solar cell by joining (a), (b) and (c).

A solar cell is an electric cell which converts sunlight into electrical energy.

Now make eight definitions using the information in this table. You must decide on the correct combinations of (a), (b) and (c).

(a)	(b)	(c)
a generator	a material	measures light
an insulator	an instrument	readily releases electrons
an alternating current	a current	flows first in one direction, then in the other
a direct current	a device	does not readily release electrons
a resistor		impedes the flow of current in a circuit
a conductor		measures current
a light meter		converts mechanical energy into electrical energy
an ammeter		flows in one direction only

EXERCISE I *Making definitions*

Try to write your own definitions of these:

1. a voltmeter
2. an electric motor
3. a receiver
4. a transmitter
5. an electric cell

EXERCISE J *Relative clauses 3: adding information to a passage*

Use non-defining relative clauses to add extra information to this paragraph about a relay. This extra information is given below the paragraph.

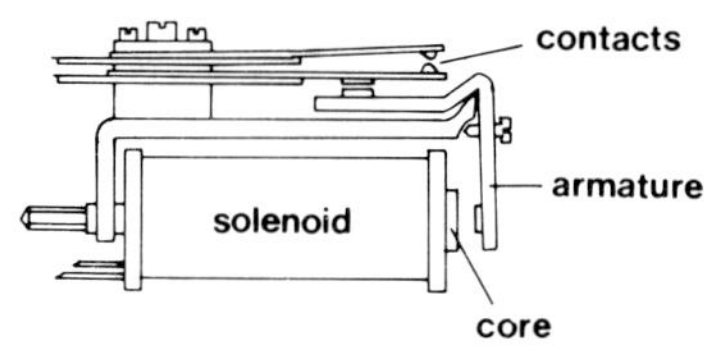

Electric relays (1). . . . . . utilize the magnetic effect of a current in a solenoid. One of the most common types (2). . . . . . consists of a solenoid with a soft-iron core. When energized by a suitable dc current, the solenoid attracts an armature (3). . . . . . The armature is pivoted in such a way that it pushes together or pulls apart a set of contacts (4). . . . . . These contacts (5). . . . . . control one or more circuits. Normally these circuits draw a much heavier current than the relay coil itself.

1. Electric relays are widely used in telecommunications.
2. The most common type of relay is known as the hinged armature relay.
3. The armature is also made of soft iron.
4. The sets of contacts are mounted on the body of the relay.
5. The contacts are often made of silver.

EXERCISE K *Qualification*

Study these sentences:

1. All metals are conductors.
2. Some metals do not conduct well.

Sentence 2 qualifies sentence 1. We can link a statement and a qualification using *however*, *but* or *although*.

EXAMPLES

1. All metals are conductors, HOWEVER some metals do not conduct well.
2. All metals are conductors BUT some do not conduct well.
3. ALTHOUGH all metals are conductors, some do not conduct well.

Link each of the statements in the left-hand column with a suitable qualification from the right-hand column.

1. The unit of capacitance is the farad.	Valves are still used in large, transmitters.
2. In an ideal transformer there would be no loss.	For high grade work a tolerance of 1 or 2% is required.
3. Moving-iron meters can measure ac voltages without a rectifier.	Capitance is usually measured in microfarads or picofarads.
4. Resistors usually have a tolerance of 5 or 10%.	In practice there is always some loss.
5. Semiconductors have replaced valves in most applications.	Moving-coil meters with rectifiers are preferred.

When we qualify a statement, it is common to give a reason for the qualification.

EXAMPLE

Mica is an excellent dielectric.	*statement*
It is not used for making large capacitors.	*qualification*
The cost would be excessive.	*reason*

Mica is an excellent dielectric but it is not used for making large capacitors because the cost would be excessive.

EXERCISE L *Giving reasons for qualification*

Add an explanation to each of the qualifications you made in Exercise K using the information below. Use *because* or *because of*. (See Unit 1, Exercise K.)

1. the resistance of the windings
2. the farad is too large a unit
3. higher standards of accuracy are needed
4. the very high powers required
5. they do not absorb so much power from the circuit

III INFORMATION TRANSFER

EXERCISE M *Terms used in electrical engineering and electronics*

Study the table of terms in Appendix 2. Then write out the following expressions in full.

1. $I = \frac{V}{R}$
2. $B \propto H$
3. $P = I^2 \times R = 40\ W$
4. $V = \frac{Q}{C} = \frac{1{\cdot}6 \times 10^{-3}}{20 \times 10^{-6}} = 80\ V$
5. $Z = \sqrt{R^2 + (X_L - X_C)^2} = 330\Omega$
6. $V = I\ \frac{1}{\omega C}$
7. $f = \frac{1}{2\pi C X_C} = 79{\cdot}5\ Hz$
8. $\gamma = \frac{1}{\rho}$
9. $f_r = \frac{1}{2\pi (LC)^{\frac{1}{2}}} = 8750\ Hz$
10. $\frac{V}{Z} = I = VY$

EXERCISE N *Describing component values*

Study this table:

Prefix	Symbol	Multiple	Example	
giga	G	10^{9}	GHz	gigahertz
mega	M	10^{6}	MΩ	megohms
kilo	k	10^{3}	kV	kilovolts
deci	d	10^{-1}	dB	decibels
milli	m	10^{-3}	mW	milliwatts
micro	μ	10^{-6}	μA	microamps
nano	n	10^{-9}	nF	nanofarads
pico	p	10^{-12}	pF	picofarads

Identify the following components in the circuit of the amplifier and write out their values in full:

1. R 4
2. R 9
3. C 5
4. C 1
5. F 1
6. L_1
7. R_L
8. R 8

EXAMPLES

R 3 A three point three ohm resistor.
C 6 A thousand microfarad electrolytic capacitor.

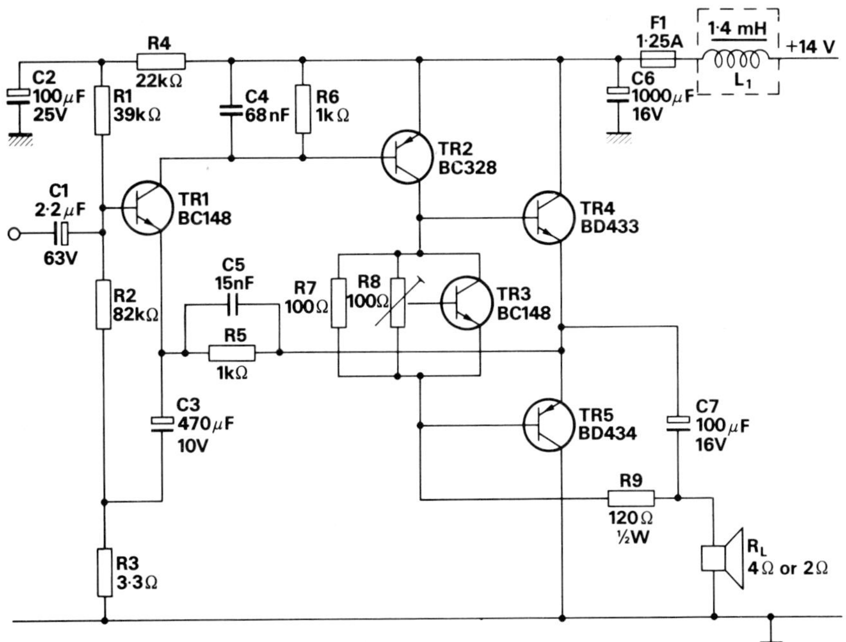

IV GUIDED WRITING

STAGE 1 *Sentence building*

Join the following groups of sentences to make ten longer sentences. Use the words printed in italics above each group. You may omit words and make whatever changes you think are necessary in the word order and punctuation of the sentences.

1. *which*
   A resistor is a device.
   A resistor is used to add resistance to a circuit.
2. *both*
   Many types of resistors are made.
   Fixed and variable resistors are made.
3. *either . . . or*
   Most resistors are made from two materials.
   Resistance wire and compressed graphite are used.
4. *such as, which*
   Wirewound resistors consist of a coil of resistance wire.
   Nichrome is a resistance wire.
   The resistance wire is wound on a former.
5. *to*
   A ceramic coating is applied over the winding.
   The ceramic coating insulates the winding.
6. *for example*
   For small currents, carbon resistors are used.
   Small currents are usual in radio work.
7. *which*
   Carbon resistors are made of compressed graphite.
   The graphite is formed into small tubes.
8. *which*
   Connections are made with wires.
   The wires are attached to the ends of the resistor.
9. *either . . . or*
   Variable resistors may have a coil of resistance wire.
   Variable resistors may have a carbon track.
10. *so that*
    The wire or track is mounted.
    A sliding contact can rub over it to select the resistance required.

STAGE 2 *Paragraph building*

Construct a paragraph from the sentences you have made in Stage 1.

STAGE 3 *Using diagrams to illustrate a passage*

Use diagrams 1 and 2 in Exercise E, Unit 3, page 30 to illustrate your paragraph. Add references to these diagrams at suitable points in your paragraph.

EXAMPLES

See Figure 2.   As shown in Figure 1.

V READING AND SUMMARIZING

STAGE 1 *Comprehension*

Study this passage carefully and answer the questions which follow:

MAGNETOHYDRODYNAMIC (MHD) GENERATION

In conventional power generation, fuel such as oil or coal is burned. The burning fuel heats boilers to produce steam. The steam is used to drive turbo-alternators. The MHD process generates electricity without requiring a boiler or a turbine.

MHD generation works on the principle that when a conductor cuts a magnetic field, a current flows through the conductor. In MHD generation the conductor is an ionized gas. Small amounts of metal are added to the gas to improve its conductivity. This is called seeding the gas. The seeded gas is then pumped at a high temperature and pressure through a strong magnetic field. The electrons in the gas are collected at an electrode. This movement of electrons constitutes a current flow.

Two methods of MHD generation can be used: the open-cycle and the closed-cycle. In the open-cycle method the hot gas is discharged. In the closed-cycle method it is recirculated.

The open-cycle method uses gas from burning coal or oil. The gas is seeded and then passed through a magnetic field to generate current. The seeding elements are recovered and the gas can then be used to drive a turbine before being allowed to escape.

The closed-cycle method uses an inert gas, such as helium, which is heated indirectly. The gas is circulated continually through the MHD generator.

MHD generation is still in its early stages but already an efficiency rate of 60% has been reached. This compares with a maximum of 40% from conventional power stations.

1. How does the MHD process differ from conventional systems?
2. What principle does MHD generation make use of?
3. What form does the conductor take in the MHD process?
4. What happens to the gas?

5. What methods of MHD generation are in use?
6. How do the two methods differ?
7. How does the efficiency of this process compare with conventional systems?

STAGE 2 *Summarizing*

Complete this summary of the passage using your answers to Stage 1:

Unlike conventional power generation, the MHD process does not require ......
It operates on the principle that ......
The conductor is an ionized gas seeded with ......
It is pumped at a high temperature and pressure ......
Two methods can be used: ......
In the open-cycle method gas from oil or coal is passed through a magnetic field and then used to drive a turbine before ......, whereas in the closed-cycle method ......
The MHD process has an efficiency rate of ...... compared with ...... for conventional stations.

Unit 3

I READING AND COMPREHENSION

THE DC MOTOR

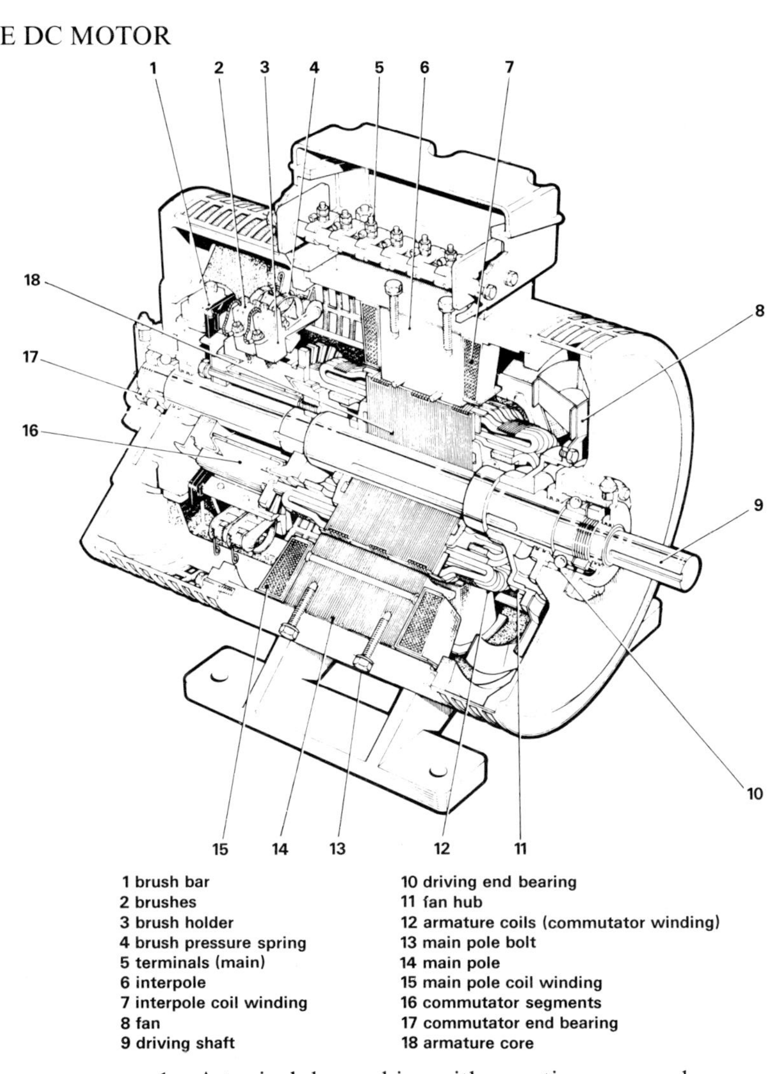

FIGURE 1 A typical dc machine with a section removed

An electric motor is a machine for converting electrical energy into mechanical energy. Motors can be designed to run on direct (dc) or alternating current (ac). The motor shown in Figure 1 is a dc motor. Its most important parts are the rotor, the stator and the brushgear.

The rotor is the moving part. It contains an armature, which is a set of wire loops wound on a steel core. When current is fed to the armature, these windings produce a magnetic field. The armature and core are mounted on a shaft which runs on bearings. It provides a means of transmitting power from the motor.

The rotor also contains a commutator. This consists of a number of copper segments insulated from one another. The armature windings are connected to these segments. Carbon brushes are held in contact with the commutator by springs. These brushes allow current to pass to the armature windings. As the rotor turns, the commutator acts as a switch making the current in the armature alternate.

The stator does not move. It consists of magnetic and electrical conductors. The magnetic circuit is made up of the frame and the poles. Wound round the poles are the field coils. These form the stator's electrical circuit. When current is fed to them, a magnetic field is set up in the stator.

The motor operates on the principle that when a current-carrying conductor is placed in a magnetic field, a force is produced on the conductor. The interaction of the forces produced by the magnetic field of the rotor and the stator makes the rotor spin.

EXERCISE A *Meaning from context*

Select the word from the three alternatives given which is most similar in meaning to the word in italics as it is used in the passage:

1. *provides* (line 8)
   (a) produces
   (b) supplies
   (c) allows

2. *segments* (line 11)
   (a) sections
   (b) pieces
   (c) wires

3. *alternate* (line 15)
   (a) reverse
   (b) change
   (c) flow in one direction then in another

4. *interaction* (line 22)
   (a) acting together
   (b) operation
   (c) result

EXERCISE B *Completing a diagram*

Complete the following diagram of the components of a dc motor using the information in the passage and Figure 1.

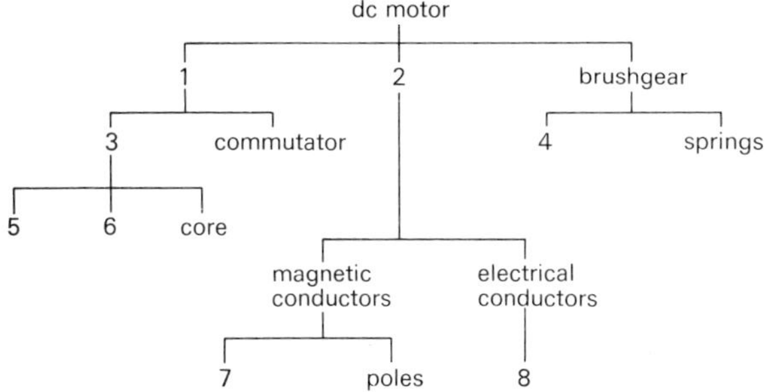

EXERCISE C *Describing position*

Describe where the following components are located using the information in the passage and Figure 1.

1. the armature windings
2. the core
3. the fan
4. the field coils
5. the poles

II USE OF LANGUAGE

EXERCISE D *Describing component parts 1*

The following verbs can be used to break down a piece of equipment into its component parts. Note how they are used.

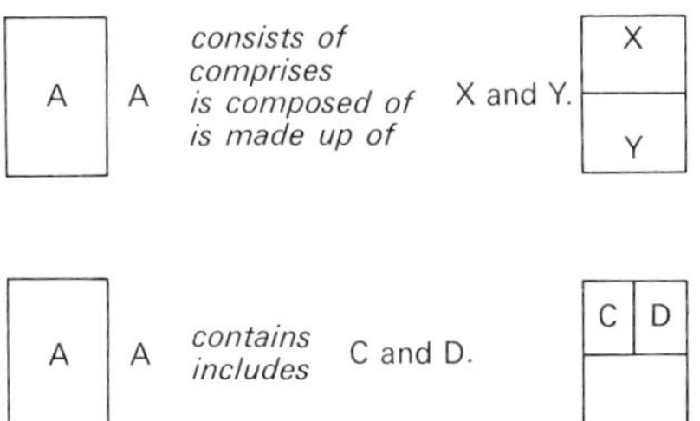

Study this description of a simple transformer:

> A simple transformer consists of two coils, a primary and a secondary, wound on a former which is mounted on a soft-iron core. The coils are made up of a number of turns of insulated wire. The core is composed of thin laminations. Either E- and I- or U- and T-shaped laminations are used. The former is mounted on the centre limb of the E or T.

Complete this diagram of the components of the transformer.

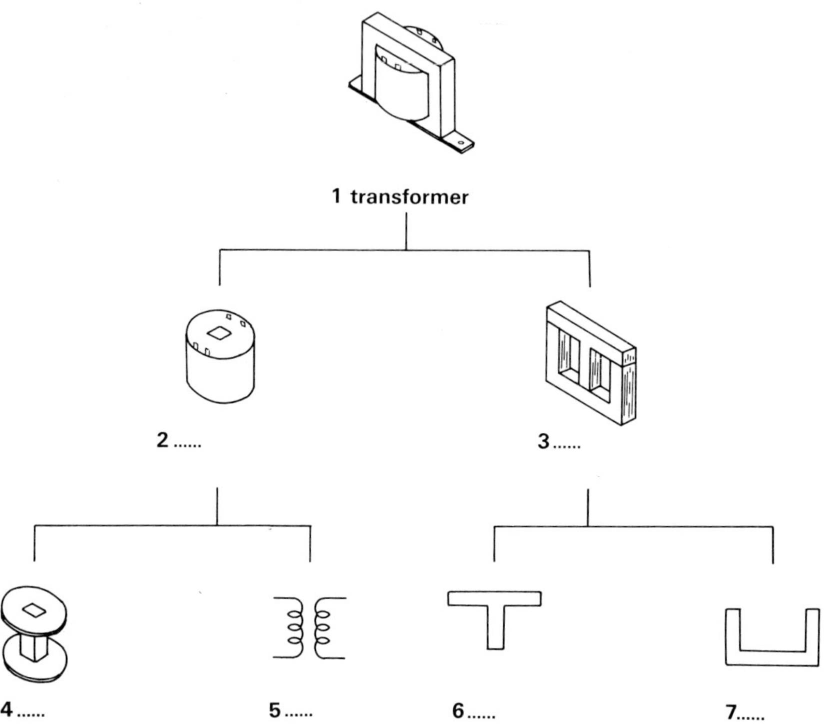

Now write your own description of a transformer using the diagram.

EXERCISE E *Describing component parts 2*

Break down each of these items into its components using the verbs you have learned. Where possible, draw a diagram to illustrate the breakdown.

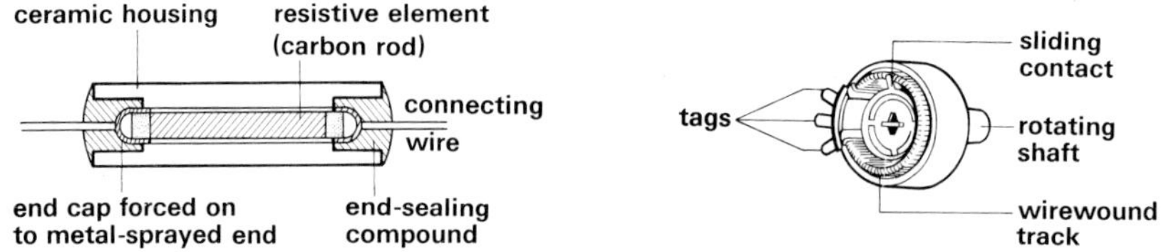

1. a carbon resistor

2. a variable wirewound resistor

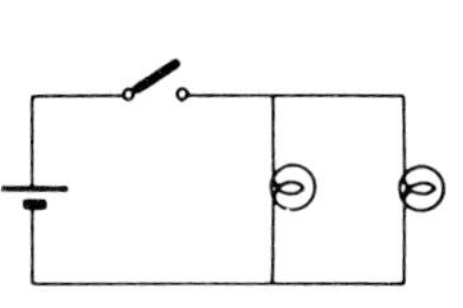

3. a lamp circuit

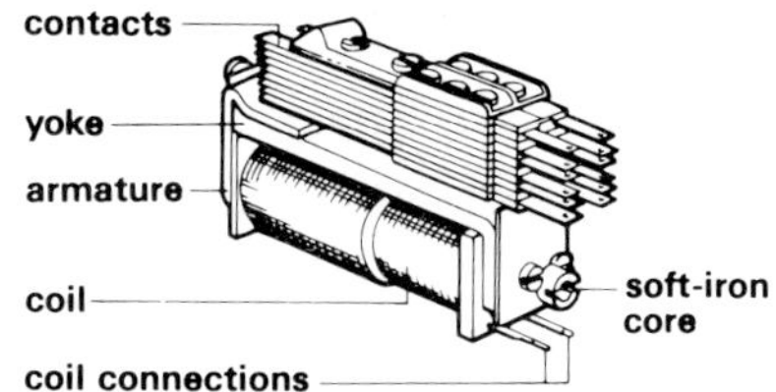

4. a relay

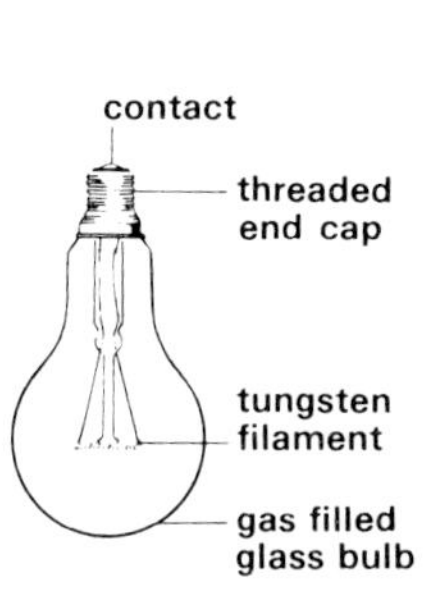

5. a filament lamp

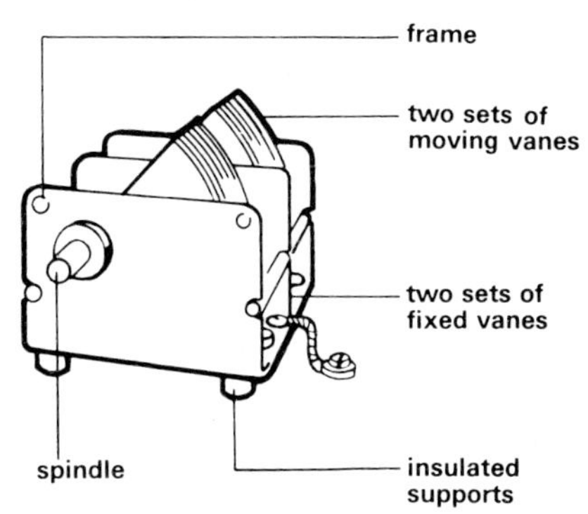

6. a variable capacitor

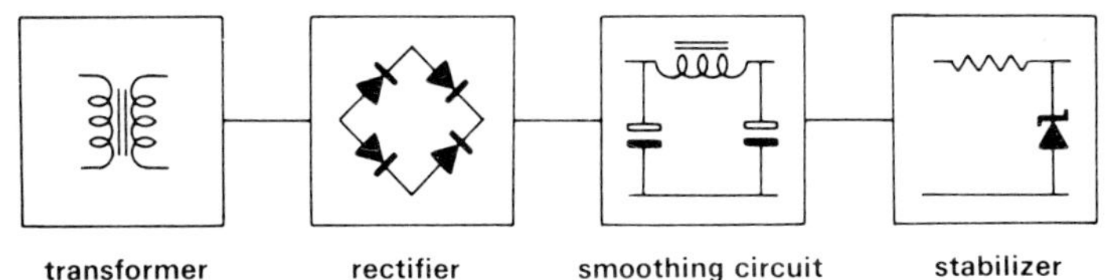

7. a power supply

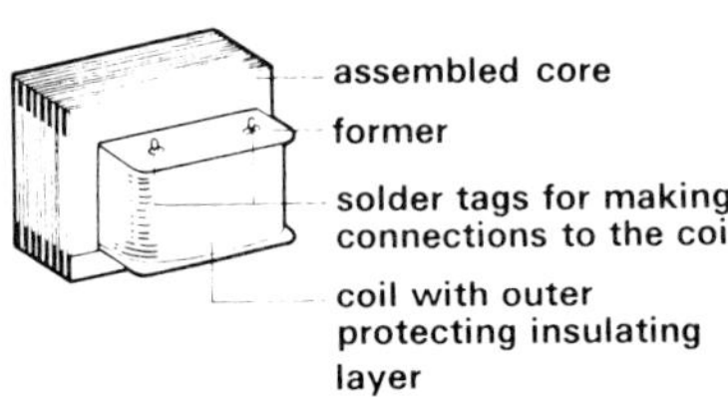

8. a choke

EXERCISE F *Writing impersonal instructions*

Study these instructions:

1. Use a high-resistance voltmeter.
2. Do not insert a fuse in an earth conductor.

In writing, instructions are often made impersonal using *should.*

EXAMPLES

1. A high-resistance voltmeter SHOULD be used.
2. A fuse SHOULD NOT be inserted in an earth conductor.

We can emphasize an instruction by using *must.*

EXAMPLES

1. A high-resistance voltmeter MUST be used.
2. A fuse MUST NOT be inserted in an earth conductor.

Here are some points to remember when using transistors. Study them:

1. Use heat shunts when soldering.
2. Do not connect or disconnect transistors with the power on.
3. Do not use an ohmmeter for checking transistors unless a safe voltage or current range is used.
4. Keep sharp bends in the leads at least 1·5 mm away from the transistor body.
5. Do not exceed the reverse breakdown voltage.

Rewrite each instruction to make it impersonal. Then emphasize each instruction using *must.*

EXERCISE G *Writing instructions for testing a dc motor*

Study this description of how dc motors are tested with a megger:

The supply should be disconnected by opening the main switch and removing the fuses. Both starter input terminals are joined together and connected to one terminal of the megohmmeter. The other lead of the megohmmeter is connected to the motor frame. The megohmmeter generator should be rotated at about 160 rpm and a reading taken.

If the resistance is found to be low, then the starter should be isolated and the test repeated on the starter alone. If the resistance is still low, then the starter coils should be checked individually until the fault is located. If the resistance of the starter is high, then the fault must lie in the motor and not in the starter. The brushes should be lifted off the commutator and the field windings and brushgear tested. If the resistance is satisfactory, then the armature only should be tested. If the resistance is low, then the field windings and brushgear should be tested separately until the fault is located.

This flow chart provides instructions for how to test a dc motor. Fill in the missing instructions with the help of the preceeding description.

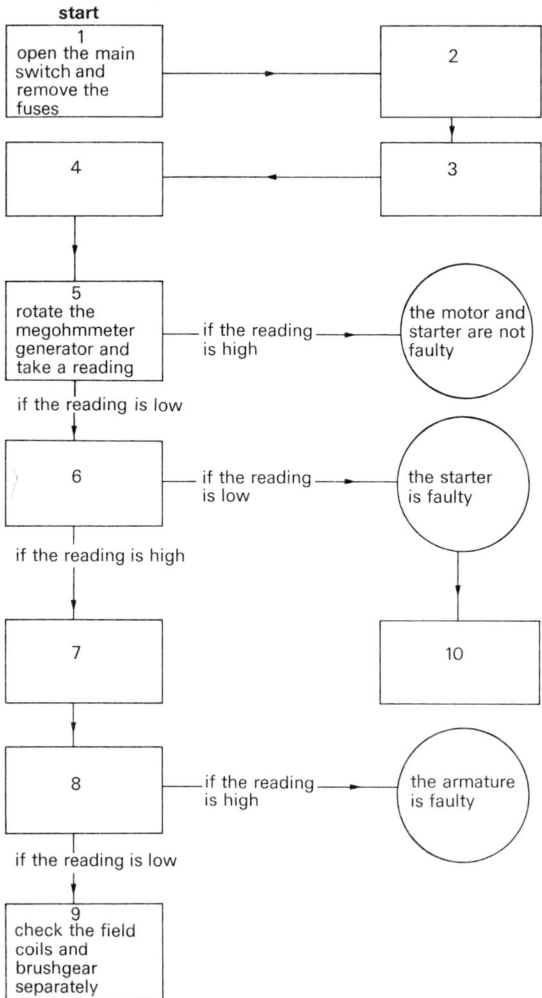

EXERCISE H *Relative clauses 4: clauses with prepositions*

Study these sentences:

1. The resistor has a value of 33 000 ohms.
2. The capacitor is connected across the resistor.

Note how they can be linked using a relative clause:

1 + 2. The resistor ACROSS WHICH THE CAPACITOR IS CONNECTED has a value of 33 000 ohms.

The repeated noun in sentence 2, *resistor*, has a preposition, *across*, before it. This preposition must be included in the relative clause. It is placed before the relative word, *which*.

Now link these sentences. Make the second sentence in each pair a relative clause. State whether the clauses are defining or non-defining. (See Unit 2, Exercise H.) Explain any difference in meaning which may occur.

1. The range is 0–1000 volts.
   The meter can operate over the range.
2. A battery is a device.
   The device changes chemical energy into electrical energy.
3. Power supplies are used to drive dc motors.
   The power supplies use thyristor rectifiers.
4. The capacitor has a value of 27pF.
   The signal is passed through the capacitor.
5. The telephone is a device.
   The device uses the magnetic effect of a current.
6. The receiver can only be used with headphones.
   The headphones have a high impedance.
7. The plates are known as X and Y plates.
   The beam passes between the plates.
8. The rotor contains a commutator.
   The commutator acts as a switch.

EXERCISE I *Reason and result connectives 2*

In Unit 1, page 8 you learned that *because* links a statement and a reason and that *therefore* links a statement and a result. The following connectives can also be used:

statement + reason

since
as
for the reason that

statement + result

hence
consequently
for this reason

If the connective has more than one syllable, use a comma before it.

EXAMPLE

Dc motors are used for cranes, for the reason that their speed can be finely controlled.

Although connectives link ideas, these ideas need not be put into one sentence.

EXAMPLE

> The current rose above the maximum. Consequently the circuit-breaker opened.

These ideas are linked by *consequently* but each is in a separate sentence.

Reason connectives, however, are almost always used to link ideas into one sentence.

EXAMPLE

> Copper is often used for cables since it is a good conductor.

Now link these ideas with either reason, result, or qualification connectives. (See Unit 1, Exercise K and Unit 2, Exercise K.)

1. Conventional current flow is from positive to negative.
   In fact electrons flow from negative to positive.
2. Alternators are preferred to dynamos for cars.
   Alternators give higher outputs at low speeds.
3. Dirt and dust reduce effective light.
   Lamps must be kept clean.
4. Squirrel-cage motors are simple, cheap and strong.
   Squirrel-cage motors are used for many general duties.
5. It is convenient to describe magnetic lines of force.
   In reality magnetic lines of force do not exist.
6. Transistorized equipment is easily portable.
   Transistors can operate from battery voltages.
7. Ultrasonic welding is better than heat welding.
   The materials are not distorted.
8. Watchmakers work with very small parts.
   Watchmakers require a lot of light.

III INFORMATION TRANSFER

EXERCISE J *Reading motor rating plates*

Study these rating plates from two electric motors:

Motor A is an induction motor of the squirrel-cage type.

HP $\frac{1}{6}$	VOLTS 240	PH 1	HZ 50
RPM 2850	AMPS 0·5	RATING Continuous	
INS CLASS E			

Motor B is a dc motor which is compound-wound.

HP 3	VOLTS 240	CYCLE dc
RPM 1400	AMPS 12	RATING Continuous
INS CLASS E		

Fill in the spaces in this table using the information given on the two motors. In the third column indicate if the features listed are the same or different. Numbers 2 and 8 have been done for you.

	Feature	Motor A	Motor B	Same or different
1.	type			
2.	horsepower	$\frac{1}{6}$	3	different
3.	volts			
4.	cycle			
5.	amps			
6.	rating			
7.	rpm			
8.	insulation class	E	E	same

EXERCISE K *Making comparisons and contrasts 1*

We can compare two similar features using *both*.

EXAMPLE

Both motors are insulation class E.

We can contrast features which are different using *whereas*.

EXAMPLE

Motor A has a horse power of $\frac{1}{6}$, *whereas* motor B has a horse power of 3.

Other words we can use for contrast are: *while, but, in contrast*. Often we can use a comparative form of an adjective to describe a difference.

EXAMPLES

Motor A rotates FASTER THAN motor B.
Motor B is MORE POWERFUL THAN motor A.

Now write sentences like the examples to compare and contrast the motors.

EXERCISE L *Making comparisons and contrasts 2*

Compare and contrast the following:

1. valves and transistors
2. alternating and direct current
3. transmitters and receivers
4. filament lamps and fluorescent tubes
5. ideal and practical transformers (See Unit 8, page 108)

IV GUIDED WRITING

STAGE 1 *Sentence building*

Join the following groups of sentences to make ten longer sentences. You may add or omit words and make whatever changes you think are necessary in the word order and punctuation of the sentences.

1. A zinc case is used as a container for the cell.
   The zinc case is used as the negative electrode.
2. A carbon rod forms the positive electrode.
   The carbon rod is in the centre of the cell.
3. The space between the zinc case and the carbon rod is filled with a paste of ammonium chloride.
   The paste is used as an electrolyte.
4. The electrolyte is a paste and not a liquid.
   This type of cell is called a dry cell.
5. The paste also contains manganese dioxide.
   The manganese dioxide prevents gas being formed.
6. The cell is sealed with a cap.
   The cap is made of metal or plastic.
   The cap is to prevent the paste coming out.
7. A small space is left below the cap.
   Gas formed by the cell can collect in the space.
8. Dry cells are usually enclosed in a cardboard case.
   An additional metal jacket may be added.
   The jacket makes the cell leakproof.
9. Leakproof cells are often preferred.
   The electrolyte cannot leak out.
   The cell ages.

10. Leaking electrolyte may damage the equipment.
    The cells are installed in the equipment.

STAGE 2 *Diagram labelling*

Label this diagram to illustrate the passage you have made with these items:

1. electrolyte
2. carbon rod
3. negative electrode
4. zinc case
5. positive electrode

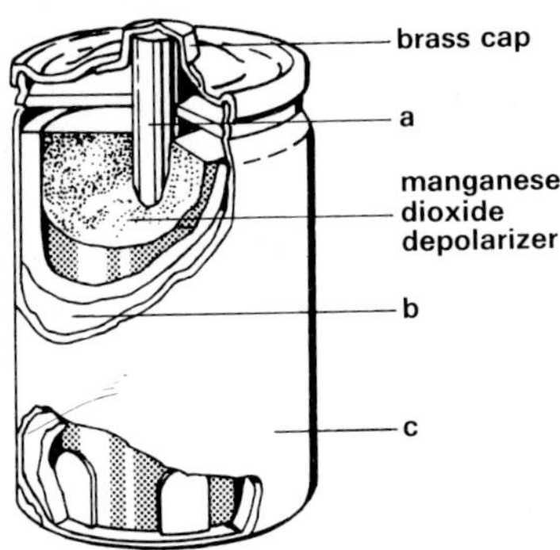

STAGE 3 *Using the diagram to illustrate the passage*

Add a reference to the diagram in your passage. Give the completed passage a suitable title.

V READING AND NOTE-TAKING

STAGE 1 *Previewing*

Read the title and the first sentence of each paragraph. Then write down what you think the passage is about.

THE EFFECTS OF AN ELECTRIC CURRENT

The effects of an electric current are thermal, luminous, chemical and magnetic. When a current flows through a conductor it may heat the conductor. This heat is sometimes undesirable and has to be reduced. For this reason many electric motors and generators contain a fan. However, domestic appliances, such as electric cookers, and many industrial processes depend on the heating effect of an electric current.

The passage of a current may produce light. This can happen in a number of ways. The heat generated by the current may be so great that the conductor becomes incandescent. For example, the filament of a light bulb emits intense white light when heated by a current. Light is also produced when a current ionizes a gas. The colour of the light will vary according to the gas used. Mercury vapour lamps give a greenish-blue light.

An electric current can separate a chemical compound into its components. This is called electrolysis. Chlorine is generated by the electrolysis of salt water. Electrolysis can also be used to break down water into hydrogen and oxygen. Because pure water does not conduct well, sulphuric acid has to be added before the electrolysis takes place.

A current flowing through a conductor creates a magnetic field around it. This field has three applications. It can magnetize magnetic materials and attract them to the conductor. The electric relay works on this principle. If the magnetic field is cut by another conductor, an electromotive force will be induced in that conductor. For instance, the change in current flowing through the primary of a transformer will induce a current in the secondary. This principle is also used in generators. Thirdly, if a current-carrying conductor is placed in the magnetic field, a force will be exerted on it. This effect is utilized in the electric motor.

STAGE 2 *Note-taking*

Now study the passage carefully and complete this framework of notes:

Effects of an electric current:
1. thermal
2. ......
3. ......
4. magnetic

1. heat can be
   (a) undesirable e.g. motor
   (b) ...... e.g. cooker
2. light
   (a) from incandescent conductor e.g. ......
   (b) from ...... e.g. vapour lamp
3. ...... = breakdown of chemical compound e.g. salt water into chlorine
4. current flowing in conductor → ...... round it. Magnetic field has 3 applications:
   (a) ...... e.g. relay
   (b) induce emf in another conductor e.g. ......
   (c) ...... e.g. motor

Unit 4

I READING AND COMPREHENSION

THE CATHODE RAY TUBE

The cathode ray tube (crt) is used in oscilloscopes, radar receivers and television sets. The type described here is that used in oscilloscopes. By means of a crt, an oscilloscope not only shows the size of a signal, but also how the signal varies with time. In other words it shows the waveform of the signal.

The crt operates as follows. First electrons are emitted from a heated cathode. Then these electrons are accelerated to give them a high velocity. Next they are formed into a beam which can be deflected vertically and horizontally. Finally they are made to strike a screen coated on its inner surface with a phosphor.

The crt comprises an electron gun and a deflection system enclosed in a glass tube with a phosphor coated screen. The electron gun forms the electrons into a beam. It contains a cathode which is heated to produce a stream of electrons. On the same axis as the cathode is a cylinder known as the grid. By varying the negative potential on the grid, the intensity of the beam can be varied. A system of three anodes follows. These accelerate the beam and also operate as a lens to focus the beam on the screen as a small dot. Varying the potential on the central anode, a_2, allows the focus to be adjusted.

On leaving the electron gun, the beam passes through two sets of plates which are at right angles to each other. The first set of plates are the Y plates. As these are nearer the anodes, they have a greater effect on the beam. Therefore the signal is applied to this set. They control the vertical deflection of the beam. The second set are the X plates. On an oscilloscope the output from a timebase oscillator is applied across these plates as a means of moving the beam horizontally at regular intervals. Hence the horizontal axis of an oscilloscope is the time axis. By means of the deflection system, then, the beam can be made to traverse the screen both horizontally and vertically.

The final element is the phosphor coated screen. When the electron beam strikes the screen, the phosphor coating fluoresces. Various colours of light are produced depending on the phosphor used.

EXERCISE A *Meaning from context*

Select a word from the three alternatives given which is most similar in meaning to the word in italics as it is used in the passage:

1. *emitted* (line 5)
   (a) scattered
   (b) given off
   (c) absorbed

2. *deflected* (line 7)
   (a) moved
   (b) bent
   (c) changed

3. *intensity* (line 14)
   (a) focus
   (b) brightness
   (c) shape

4. *adjusted* (line 17)
   (a) reduced
   (b) varied
   (c) increased

5. *regular* (line 24)
   (a) frequent
   (b) equally timed
   (c) varying

6. *fluoresces* (line 28)
   (a) lights
   (b) emits electrons
   (c) turns green

EXERCISE B *Diagram labelling*

Complete the labelling of this diagram of a cathode ray tube using the information in the passage:

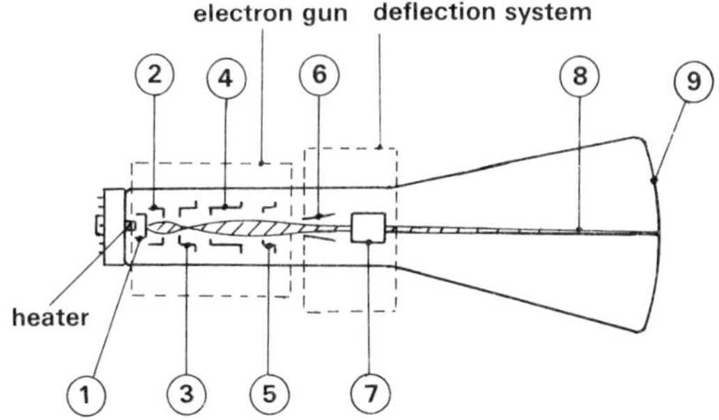

EXERCISE C *Finding out facts*

Answer these questions about the passage:

1. Why is an oscilloscope better than a meter?
2. What is the source of electrons for the electron beam?
3. What is the function of the electron gun?
4. How is the intensity of the beam controlled?
5. In what way is the system of anodes like a lens?
6. Why is the signal applied to the Y plates?
7. What does the timebase do?
8. Why is the horizontal axis of an oscilloscope the time axis?

II USE OF LANGUAGE

EXERCISE D *Describing a process*

Study these instructions for soldering a resistor into a printed circuit board (pcb):

1. Bend the leads and insert them through the correct holes in the pcb.
2. Pull the resistor flat against the board and bend back the leads.
3. Heat the first lead with a soldering iron and apply solder to the heated lead.
4. Heat and apply solder to the second lead.
5. Allow the soldered joints to cool.
6. Trim the leads using wire clippers.

Write a description of this process by rewriting each instruction in the present passive.

EXAMPLE

1. The leads are bent and inserted through the correct holes in the pcb.

EXERCISE E *Describing sequence 1: sequence words*

To make the correct sequence of a number of events clear, we often use sequence words like these:

(a) first
(b) then
(c) next
(d) after that
(e) finally

(a) and (e) must come first and last respectively, but the others can be used in any order and can be repeated.

Now replace each number in your description of soldering a resistor into a pcb with a sequence word to make the order of events clear.

EXAMPLE

First the leads are bent and inserted through the correct holes in the pcb.

EXERCISE F *Describing the distribution of power*

The following diagram shows the distribution of power from the power station to the consumer. The sentences which follow it describe this distribution. Put the sentences in the correct order and mark this order using sequence words.

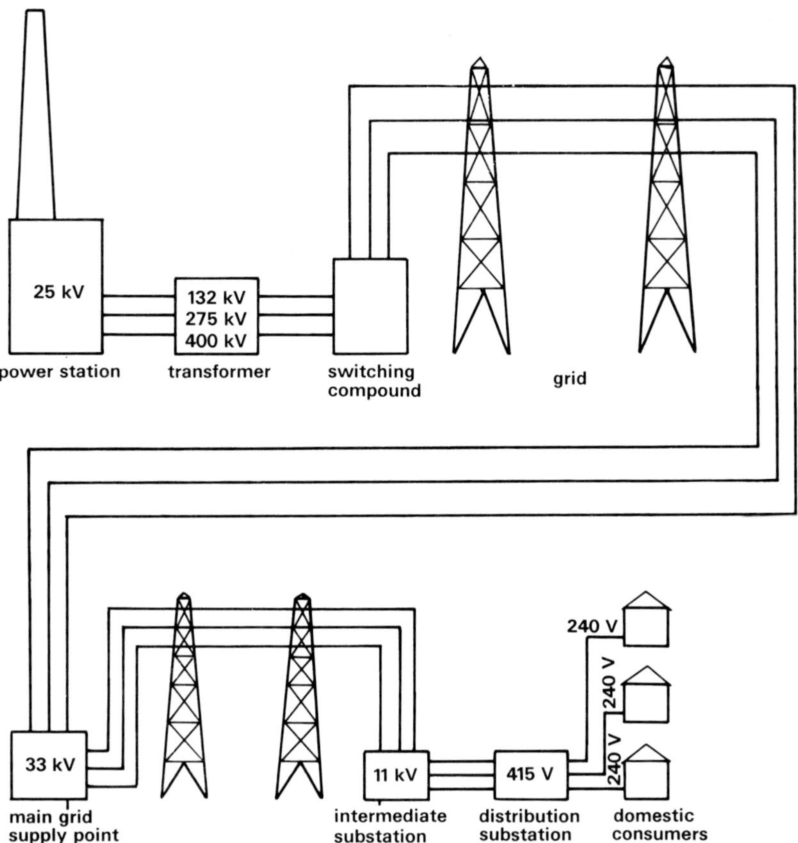

(a) It is fed to distribution substations where it is reduced to 415 V, 3 phase and 240 V, 1 phase.
(b) It is stepped up by a transformer to 132, 275 or 400 kV for long-distance distribution.
(c) It is distributed via the grid system to main grid supply points where it is stepped down to 33 kV for distribution to heavy industry.
(d) It is distributed to the domestic consumer.
(e) In the UK, electrical energy is generated at power stations at 25 kV.
(f) It passes via the switching compound to the grid.
(g) It is distributed via overhead or underground cables to intermediate substations where it is further reduced to 11 kV for light industry.

EXERCISE G *Writing instructions as explanations*

Study these instructions. They explain how to disconnect the supply to the motor in the circuit.

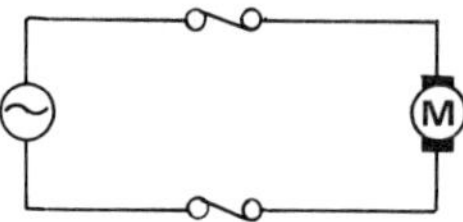

1. Disconnect the supply BY WITHDRAWING THE FUSES.
2. TO DISCONNECT the supply, WITHDRAW the fuses.

Now write instructions like the examples above to explain how to do the following:

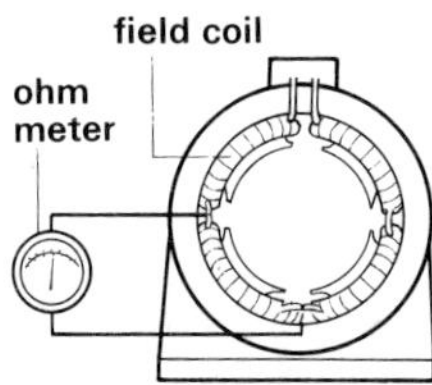

1. Check the field coils.

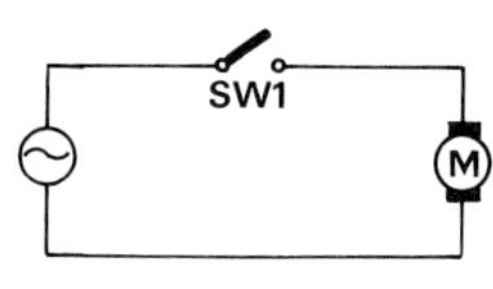

2. Start the motor.

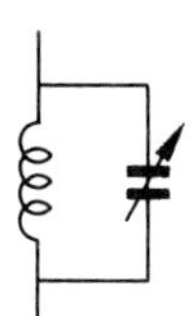

3. Change the frequency of the tuned circuit.

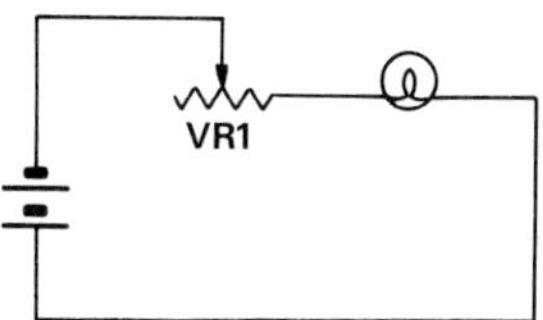

4. Dim the light.

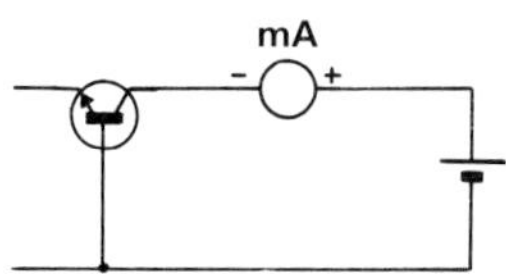

5. Measure the collector current.

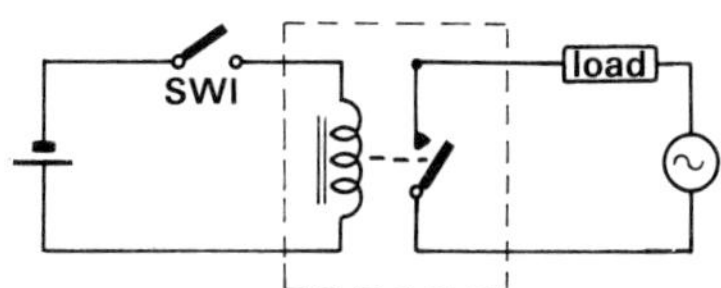

6. Supply power to the load.

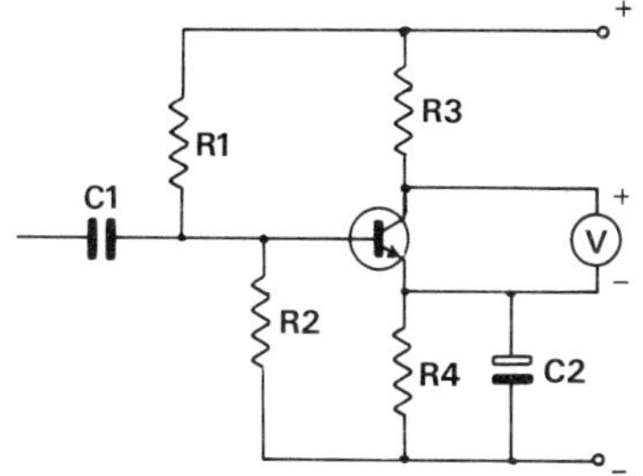

7. Measure the collector-emitter voltage.

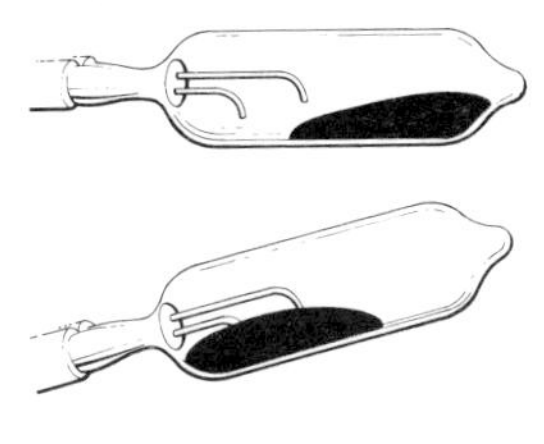

8. Operate the mercury relay.

EXERCISE H *Short relative clauses 1*

We can join these sentences by using a relative clause.

1. The lines are arranged in two groups.
2. The lines carry the supply.

1+2. The lines WHICH CARRY THE SUPPLY are arranged in two groups.

Relative clauses with certain active verbs can be shortened by omitting the relative word and changing the verb to its *-ing* form. These verbs include:

carry	form
contain	hold
consist of	measure

We can shorten the relative clause like this:

The lines CARRYING THE SUPPLY are arranged in two groups.

Note how these two sentences are joined by a relative clause.

3. The lines are suspended from insulators.
4. The insulators are made of porcelain.

3+4. The lines are suspended from insulators WHICH ARE MADE OF PORCELAIN.

Relative clauses like this with passive verbs can be shortened by omitting the relative word and the verb *to be*:

The lines are suspended from insulators MADE OF PORCELAIN.

Now link each group of sentences into one sentence. Use short relative clauses where possible. Number 2 cannot be shortened.

1. In Britain electrical energy is fed to the National Grid.
   The energy is generated in power stations.
2. The energy passes through a transformer.
   The transformer steps up the voltage to 132, 275, or 400 kV.
3. The transmission lines are usually arranged in groups of three overhead conductors.

The lines carry the supply.
The overhead conductors are suspended from porcelain insulators.

4. Energy from power stations may be fed to the Grid by underground cables.
The power stations are located in built-up areas.
5. For voltages up to 400 kV cables are used.
These cables contain oil under low pressure.

EXERCISE I *Reinforcement connectives*

Study these sentences:

1. Steel-cored aluminium is used for high-voltage lines.
2. Steel-cored aluminium lines are cheaper than copper.

Sentence 2 provides a reason for Sentence 1. We can link the ideas in these sentences with *because*.

1+2. Steel-cored aluminium is used for high-voltage lines BECAUSE it is cheaper than copper.

Now consider this sentence:

3. Steel-cored aluminium lines are 50% stronger than copper.

Sentence 3 provides an additional reason for Sentence 1. It reinforces Sentence 2. We can link a reinforcing idea using *in addition*, *moreover* or *furthermore*.

1+2+3. Steel-cored aluminium is used for high-voltage lines BECAUSE it is cheaper than copper. IN ADDITION, steel-cored aluminium lines are 50% stronger than copper.

Each group of the sentences which follow contains one statement and two supporting reasons. Identify them, then link them with appropriate connectives. Make sure repeated nouns are changed into pronouns.

1. (a) Semiconductors are cheaper than valves.
(b) Semiconductors are much smaller and lighter.
(c) Semiconductors are used in preference to valves.
2. (a) Dc motors permit powerful dynamic braking.
(b) Dc motors are preferred for cranes.
(c) Dc motors allow a wide range of speed variation.
3. (a) Dielectric heating is even.
(b) Dielectric heating is faster and cheaper.
(c) Dielectric heating rather than conduction heating is used in plywood production.
4. (a) Fluorescent lamps are better than filament lamps.
(b) The light is closer to daylight.
(c) The heat from fluorescent lamps is much less than from filament lamps.

EXERCISE J *Reinforcing ideas in a passage*

Fill the spaces in this paragraph with suitable reinforcing ideas from the table.

A number of instruments can be employed to measure voltage. The moving-coil multimeter is often used because it is cheap and reasonably accurate. Moreover (1). . . . . However if the impedance of the instrument is low, the meter will draw too much current from the circuit. In addition, (2). . . . . . The electronic voltmeter is almost ideal since the circuit is not loaded. Furthermore (3). . . . . . However it is a relatively expensive instrument. The electrostatic meter is the simplest instrument for very high voltages. It responds to both ac and dc. However it is insensitive and (4). . . . . . The cathode ray oscilloscope gives more information than any other instrument. It not only measures the voltage but it also (5). . . . . . However oscilloscopes are usually large. In addition, (6). . . . . .

Instruments for voltage measurement

Instrument	Advantages	Disadvantages
Moving-coil multimeter	reasonably accurate, robust, versatile	frequency range limited on ac
Electronic voltmeter	draws no current from the circuit, wide frequency range	expensive
Electrostatic meter	simple, can be used with ac or dc without a rectifier	insensitive, has a non-linear scale
Oscilloscope	also gives information about waveform and frequency	large, expensive

III INFORMATION TRANSFER

EXERCISE K *Reading a diagram 1*

Study this diagram of a moving-coil meter:

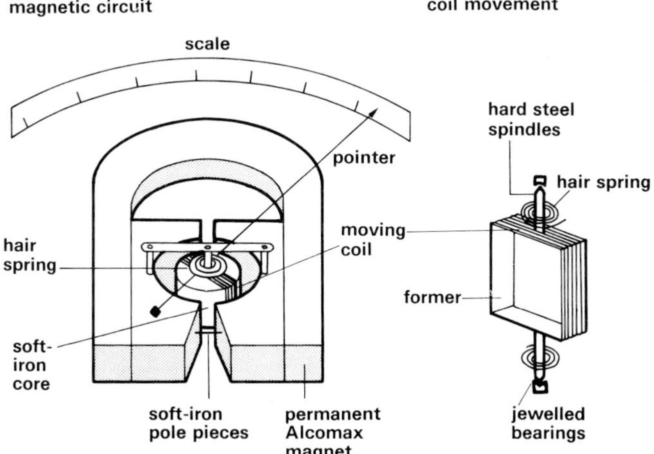

Now complete this table using the information in the diagram:

	component	shape	material
1.	magnet	U-shaped	
2.		curved	soft-iron
3.	core		
4.	former		aluminium
5.		pointed	hard-steel
6.		spiral	phosphor bronze

EXERCISE L *Making compound nominal groups*

Compound nominal groups are common in technical writing.

EXAMPLES

1. a phosphor-coated screen
2. a current-carrying conductor
3. a printed circuit board

Many different types of information are combined in such groups. In this section we will study groups which combine information on the shape and the materials from which an object is made.

Use the table you completed in Exercise K to make compound nominal groups.

EXAMPLE

1. 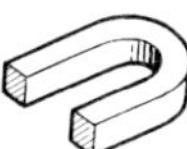 A U-shaped Alcomax magnet.

EXERCISE M *Reading a diagram 2*

Using the diagram of the moving-coil meter on page 47, fill in the spaces in this description of the meter. The nominal groups you made in Exercise L and the position and connection phrases you studied in Unit 1, Exercise E will help you.

The essential components of a moving-coil meter are a . . . . . . and a moving-coil. The magnet is . . . . . . or semi-circular and is made of a material such as Alcomax. Each pole terminates in a . . . . . . pole piece. The . . . . . . which gives the instrument its name is composed of fine copper wire . . . . . . a thin rectangular . . . . . .   The former is mounted centrally on hard steel . . . . . .

and can rotate around a fixed cylindrical . . . . . .   The core is . . . . . . the pole pieces in such a way that an annular gap is formed between it and the pole pieces. A pointer is . . . . . . the former and traverses a linear scale.

Compare your answers with the opening paragraphs of the reading passage in Unit 5 on page 52.

IV GUIDED WRITING

STAGE 1 *Interpreting a diagram*

Study this diagram of a simple radar system. Column A describes the components and how they are related. Column B lists the stages in the operation of the system in sequence.

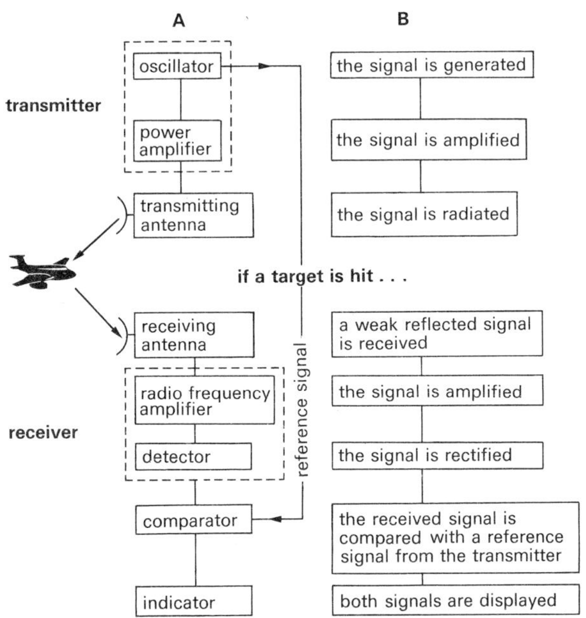

Answer these questions about the diagram:

1. What does a simple radar system consist of?
2. What does the transmitter comprise?
3. What does the receiver include?

4. Where is the signal generated?
5. What happens to the signal next?
6. How is the transmitter signal radiated?
7. If a target is hit, what receives the reflected signal?
8. Where is the signal then fed to?
9. What happens to the signal in the receiver?
10. Where is the signal fed to next?
11. What happens in the comparator?
12. What happens to both signals finally?

STAGE 2 *Describing a diagram*

Use your answers to the questions in Stage 1 to write a description of a simple radar system.

V READING AND NOTE-TAKING

STAGE 1 *Previewing*

Read the title and the first sentence of each paragraph. Then write down what you think the passage is about.

DIELECTRIC HEATING

Dielectric heating is a method of heating a non-conducting material, a dielectric, by high-frequency voltages. The material is placed between metal plates across which a high-frequency supply is connected as shown in Figure 1. The dielectric and the plates then form a capacitor and an electrostatic field is set up in the dielectric. As very high frequencies are used, up to 200 MHz, the movement of electrons in the dielectric becomes rapid. This causes considerable heat in the substance.

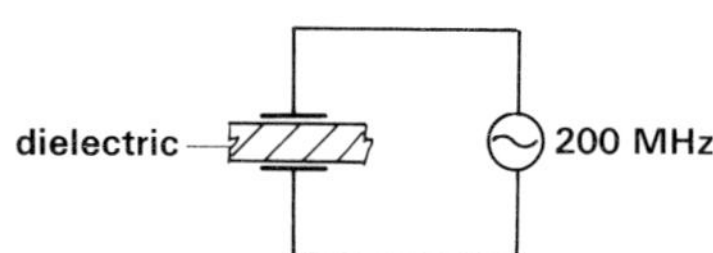

Dielectric heating has two great advantages over other forms of heating: it provides rapid heat, and the heat is produced uniformly throughout the material. In other words, the inside of the material gets hot at the same time as the surface. In addition, dielectric heating can be easily controlled and it is predictable. Accurate heating times can be calculated knowing the dielectric properties of the materials to be heated.

Dielectric heating has many different uses, from the manufacture of plastic raincoats to baking biscuits. It is especially used in plastics, woodworking and food industries.

A typical use is the manufacture of plywood. In the past the layers of wood and glue were steam-heated under pressure until the glue melted and the wood was firmly bonded. The heat took a long time to penetrate the wood, the glue did not melt uniformly and it dried unevenly. With dielectric heating, because of the difference in dielectric properties, the glue melts before the wood heats. It heats uniformly and it dries evenly. Using the dielectric process, a single press can prepare 100 3-ply, 1 cm thick sheets of plywood in about 30 minutes.

STAGE 2 *Note-taking*

Now study the passage carefully and complete this framework of notes:

Dielectric heating
Dielectric heating = hf heating of . . . . . .

Operation
Materials and electrodes form a capacitor.
Hf voltage applied to electrodes → rapid electron movement → . . . . . .

Advantages
Heat is
1. . . . . . .
2. . . . . . .
3. controllable and predictable

Applications
1. plastics e.g. raincoats
2. . . . . . .
3. . . . . . . e.g. biscuits

Example – plywood
Old, steamheat BUT
1. lengthy
2. . . . . . .
3. . . . . . .
New, dielectric
1. glue melts before wood heats
2. . . . . . .
3. . . . . . .

When you have completed your notes, try to read them back in complete sentences.

Unit 5

I READING AND COMPREHENSION

THE MOVING-COIL METER

1. Construction and components

The essential components of a moving-coil meter are a permanent magnet and a moving coil. The magnet is U-shaped or semi-circular and is made of a material such as Alcomax. Each pole terminates in a soft-iron pole piece, shaped and positioned as in Figure 1.

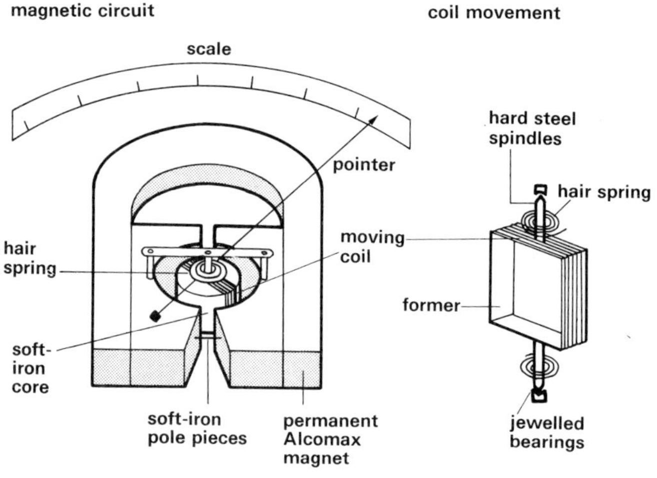

FIGURE 1

The moving coil, which gives the instrument its name, is composed of fine copper wire wound on a thin rectangular aluminium former. The former is mounted centrally on hard steel spindles and can rotate around a fixed cylindrical soft-iron core. The core is placed between the pole pieces in such a manner that an annular gap is formed between it and the pole pieces. A pointer is attached to the former and traverses a linear scale.

The spindles which bear the moving coil are mounted on jewelled bearings. Two spiral hair springs are attached to the spindles. They are wound in opposition and are adjusted so that they balance when the pointer is at the zero mark on the scale.

2. Operation

This instrument operates on the principle that when a current carrying conductor is placed in a magnetic field, a force is exerted on the conductor which causes it to move.

When the meter is inserted in a live circuit, current flows through the control springs into the coil. This sets up a magnetic field around the coil which reacts with the radial magnetic field of the permanent magnet. The reaction produces a torque which tends to rotate the coil. Since the strength of the permanent magnet's field is uniform, this torque is directly proportional to the current flowing in the coil. As the coil rotates, the control springs oppose the motion of the coil. When the deflecting force of the coil is balanced by the controlling force of the springs, the coil comes to rest. The extent of the coil's movement, and hence the size of the current flowing through the coil, is indicated on the scale by the pointer.

EXERCISE A *Describing position*

Say where the following components are located. Use the expressions you learned in Unit 1, Exercise E:

1. the pole pieces
2. the core
3. the pointer
4. the former
5. the springs

EXERCISE B *Describing function*

This table describes the function of the components of the meter. The functions are in the wrong order. Write a sentence to describe the function of each component using the methods you learned in Unit 2, Exercise D. Note that the springs have two functions.

	component	function
1.	core	to provide controlling torque
2.	former	to reduce friction and wear
3.	springs	to produce a powerful uniform magnetic field
4.	bearings	to carry the coil
5.	magnet	to serve as leads to carry current to the coil
		to produce radial field lines within the gap

Now add to Part 1 of the reading passage a description of the function of these components. Begin like this:

> The function of the moving-coil meter is to detect the presence of a direct current. Its essential components . . . . . .

EXERCISE C *Rephrasing*

Rewrite the following sentences replacing the words in italics with expressions from the passage which have a similar meaning:

1. The meter is inserted in *a circuit with a current flowing through it.*
2. The coil is rotated by a *turning force.*
3. The strength of the permanent magnet's field is *always the same.*
4. The turning force *varies directly with* the current flowing through the coil.
5. *The force which rotates the coil* is balanced by the *force which restrains the coil.*

EXERCISE D *Making deductions*

Part 2 of the reading passage is an explanation. It tells us the answers to several questions.

EXAMPLE

> Why does the coil rotate?

To understand this explanation, you must be able to make deductions from information in the passage. In addition, you must be able to contribute information of your own to help you to understand some parts of the passage.

Try to complete the following deductions. Each consists of two sentences which contain information – (a) and (b). From these you can make a deduction (c).

EXAMPLE

(a) When a current flows through a conductor, a magnetic field is set up round the conductor.
(b) A current flows through the meter coil when it is inserted in a circuit.
∴ (c) *A magnetic field is set up round the meter coil.*

1. (a) When a current-carrying conductor is placed in a magnetic field, a force is exerted on it.
   (b) The coil carries current and is in the magnetic field of the permanent magnet.
   ∴ (c) A force . . . . . .
2. (a) A radial magnetic field produces rotation.
   (b) Because of the pole pieces and the core, the magnetic field of the meter is radial.
   ∴ (c) The coil . . . . . .

3. (a) The force on a current-carrying conductor in a magnetic field is directly proportional to the current and the strength of the magnetic field.
   (b) The strength of the magnetic field of the permanent magnet does not vary.
∴ (c) The rotating force . . . . . .
4. (a) As the coil rotates, the control springs oppose the motion of the coil.
   (b) This makes it increasingly difficult for the coil to turn.
∴ (c) The coil . . . . . .

II USE OF LANGUAGE

EXERCISE E *Cause and effect 1*

Study this sentence:

Insulation breakdown leads to short circuits.

This sentence contains a cause and effect. We can link a cause and an effect as follows:

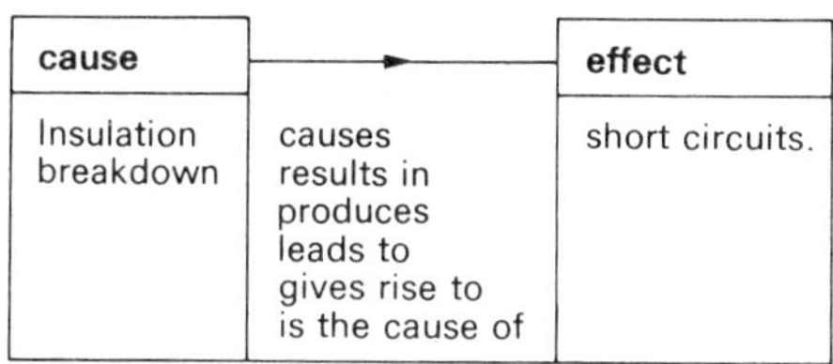

cause	→	effect
Insulation breakdown	causes results in produces leads to gives rise to is the cause of	short circuits.

We can also put the effect first:

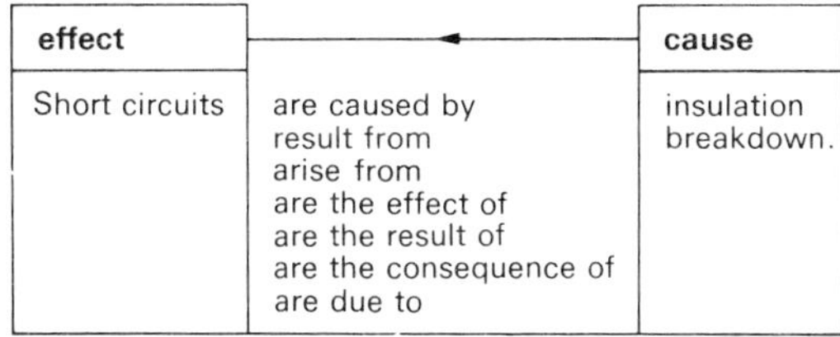

effect	←	cause
Short circuits	are caused by result from arise from are the effect of are the result of are the consequence of are due to	insulation breakdown.

When a cause has several effects or when an effect has a number of possible causes, we put *can* or *may* before the causative expression.

EXAMPLES

Sparking MAY be caused by worn brushes.
Sparking CAN be caused by a worn commutator.

Similarly, instead of *the* cause/effect/result/consequence of, we write *one* cause/effect/result/consequence of.

EXAMPLES

Worn brushes are ONE cause of sparking.
A worn commutator is ONE cause of sparking.

Now match these cause and effect pairs. Then link them using the expressions given above. Write two sentences for each example, one with the cause first and the other with the effect first.

	CAUSE	EFFECT
1.	glare	arcing across the points
2.	eddy currents	power losses in transformers
3.	excessive heat	serious accidents
4.	faulty soldering	breakdown of the motor
5.	sparking	discomfort to the eyes
6.	failure of a points capacitor	damage to semiconductors
7.	exceeding the motor rating	bad joints
8.	faulty earth connections	interference in receivers

EXERCISE F *Cause and effect chains*

Describe this cause and effect chain. Use a different expression for each link.

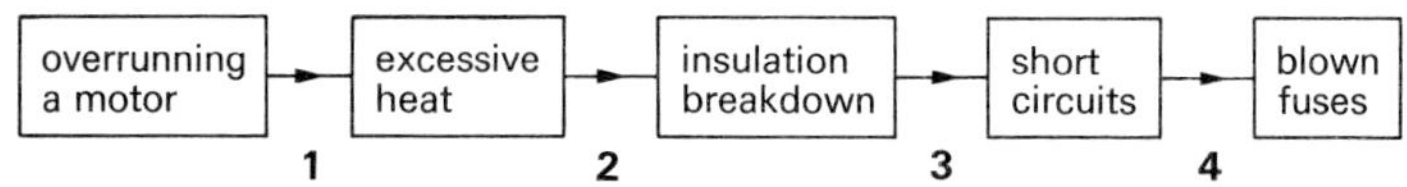

Now rewrite your description starting at the end of the chain and working backwards.

EXERCISE G *Describing sequence 2: time clauses*

Study this list of events in the manufacture of carbon resistors:

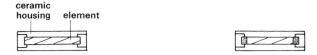

1. The resistive element is inserted into the ceramic housing.
2. The ends of the element are sprayed with metal.

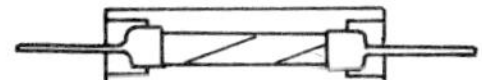

3. End caps and leads are forced on to the sprayed ends.

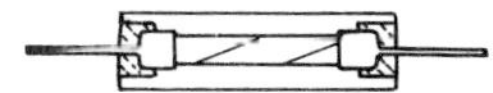

4. The ends of the resistor are sealed.

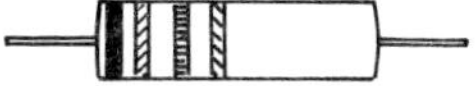

5. The value is marked on the housing.

As you learned in Unit 4, Exercise E, we can show that event 2 followed event 1 by using sequence words.

EXAMPLE

FIRST the resistive element is inserted into the ceramic housing. THEN the ends of the element are sprayed with metal.

We can also show sequence by using time clauses.

EXAMPLES

AFTER THE RESISTIVE ELEMENT IS INSERTED INTO THE CERAMIC HOUSING, the ends are sprayed with metal.

BEFORE THE ENDS OF THE ELEMENT ARE SPRAYED WITH METAL, it is inserted into the housing.

The part of each sentence in capitals is a time clause.

Time clauses can also be put last in a sentence. When this happens, there is no comma between the time clause and the rest of the sentence.

EXAMPLE

The ends of the element are sprayed with metal AFTER IT IS INSERTED INTO THE CERAMIC HOUSING.

Now write sentences linking these events with time clauses using the time word given:

1. After 2, 3.
2. 3 before 4.
3. 5 after 4.

EXERCISE H *Describing the reception of a signal*

Put these events, which describe the progress of a signal through a receiver, in sequence with the help of the diagram. Then link the sentences in pairs using time clauses with *before* and *after*.

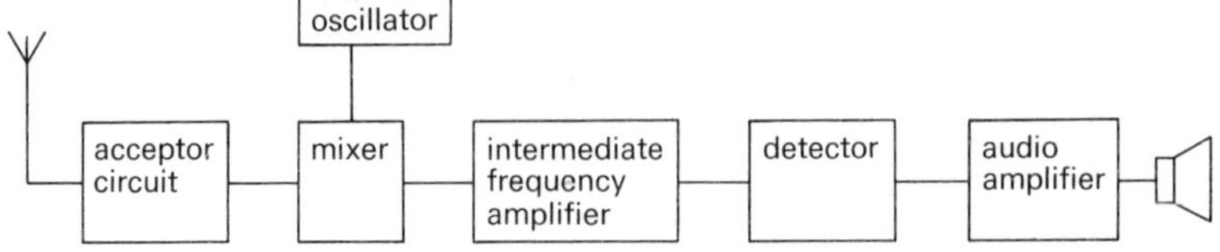

(a) the signal is again amplified
(b) the desired signal is fed to the acceptor circuit
(c) the signal is amplified
(d) the signal is fed to a loudspeaker
(e) the signal is mixed with a signal from the oscillator to give a standard intermediate frequency
(f) the signal is rectified by the detector.

EXERCISE I *Describing sequence 3: reduced time clauses*

Study these two events in the manufacture of dry cells:

1. The cell is sealed.
2. The cell is cased with a metal skin.

We can show that event 2 follows event 1 using a time clause:

AFTER THE CELL IS SEALED, it is cased with a metal skin.

The subject of the time clause, *the cell*, is the same as the subject of the main clause, *it*. When this happens we can rewrite the time clause using the *-ing* part of the verb:

AFTER BEING SEALED, the cell is cased with a metal skin.

Now rewrite these sentences reducing the time clause in all those sentences where both subjects are the same. Not all the time clauses can be reduced.

1. After the resistors are sorted, they are marked to indicate their values.
2. Before you service an oscilloscope, you should discharge all large electrolytic capacitors.
3. Immediately after the pulse is transmitted, the antenna switch is closed to the receiver.
4. Before the signal is applied to the Y plates, it must be amplified.
5. The signal is amplified after it is rectified.
6. Before the operator signs off, he repeats his call sign.

EXERCISE J *Sequence in instructions*

Study these instructions:

1. Switch off the main supply.
2. Remove the fuses.

We can show the correct sequence of these instructions using short time clauses.

EXAMPLES

1. BEFORE REMOVING THE FUSES, switch off the main supply.
2. AFTER SWITCHING OFF THE MAIN SUPPLY, remove the fuses.
3. HAVING SWITCHED OFF THE MAIN SUPPLY, remove the fuses.

Now study these instructions for switching on and using an oscilloscope:

1. Set the controls in the recommended positions.
2. Switch on.
3. Allow a few minutes to warm up.
4. Advance the brightness control until the trace appears.
5. Centralize the trace with the X and Y shift controls.
6. Adjust the focus control for a clear, sharp trace.
7. Switch to the ac input.
8. Connect the input leads.
9. Increase the Y gain control to obtain a convenient size of waveform.
10. Adjust the timebase controls to obtain a clear waveform.

Now link pairs of instructions using short time clauses.

EXAMPLE

2+3. HAVING SWITCHED ON, allow a few minutes to warm up.

EXERCISE K *Short relative clauses 2*

Study these sentences:

1. A telephone dial consists of a rotatable plate.
2. The plate has ten finger holes in it.

We can link them using a relative clause:

1+2. A telephone dial consists of a rotatable plate WHICH HAS TEN FINGER HOLES IN IT.

We can shorten the relative clause in two ways:

A telephone dial consists of a rotatable plate HAVING ten finger holes in it.
A telephone dial consists of a rotatable plate WITH ten finger holes in it.

Sometimes we can reduce a relative clause to an adjective.

EXAMPLE

3. High quality instruments use resistors.
4. The resistors are wirewound.

3+4. High quality instruments use resistors WHICH ARE WIREWOUND.
High quality instruments use WIREWOUND resistors.

Make this paragraph shorter by reducing the relative clauses. Use all the methods of reduction you have learned in this unit, in Unit 4, Exercise H and Unit 5, Exercise K.

> The telephone is an instrument which enables us to transmit speech via wires. The body of the telephone contains an induction coil, capacitors, resistors, contacts, a regulator, which controls the sensitivity of the instrument, and a bell. The handset contains a microphone and a receiver which are enclosed by screwed caps at the ends of the handset. The bell contains a hammer which is operated by a solenoid. The hammer is set between two domes which are eccentrically mounted. The dial is mounted on the face of the telephone. It consists of a rotatable plate which has ten finger holes in it. A wheel, which has ten slots cut in its edge which match the finger holes, is fitted below the dial. When the plate is turned, the wheel causes spring contacts to open and close a number of times which correspond to the number dialled. This transmits pulses down the line causing selectors, which connect the calling line to the line which is called, to operate.

III INFORMATION TRANSFER

EXERCISE L *Scanning tables*

When you use reference materials, you must learn to find information quickly. *Scanning* consists of ignoring information which is irrelevant so that you can find the information you want quickly. Write down the total time you take to find the answers to these questions. Each question number refers to one of the tables below:

1. What is the recommended minimum illumination level in a hospital operating room?
2. What term is given to a wave of 15 MHz?
3. What is the rotor speed, once slip has been deducted, for a four-pole induction motor running on a 50 Hz supply?
4. What is the resistivity of nickel?
5. Which material has a dielectric constant of 7?

1. Minimum illumination levels for hospitals

	lux
wards	30
waiting rooms	70
operating table	3000
operating room	300
laboratories	200

2.

Frequency range	Wavelength range	Term
3 to 30 kHz	100 to 10 km	Very-low frequency (VLF)
30 to 300 kHz	10 to 1 km	Low frequency (LF)
300 kHz to 3 MHz	1 km to 100 m	Medium frequency (MF)
3 to 30 MHz	100 to 10 m	High frequency (HF)
30 to 300 MHz	10 to 1 m	Very-high frequency (VHF)
300 MHz to 3 GHz	1 m to 10 cm	Ultra-high frequency (UHF)
3 to 30 GHz	10 to 1 cm	Super-high frequency (SHF)

3. Synchronous speed and rotor speed at 4% slip for induction motors

No. of poles on stator	Synchronous speed on 50 Hz, rev/min	Rotor speed at 4% slip, rev/min
2	3000	2880
4	1500	1440
6	1000	960
8	750	720
10	600	576

4. Specific resistances at 20°C

material	resistivity Ωm
silver	$1{\cdot}64 \times 10^{-8}$
copper	$1{\cdot}72 \times 10^{-8}$
aluminium	$2{\cdot}82 \times 10^{-8}$
tungsten	$5{\cdot}0 \times 10^{-8}$
brass	$6{\cdot}6 \times 10^{-8}$
nickel	$6{\cdot}9 \times 10^{-8}$
manganin	$44{\cdot}0 \times 10^{-8}$
porcelain	2×10^{13}
mica	9×10^{13}

5. Values of dielectric constant for different materials

air	1
paper	2
shellac	3
mica	7
rubber	2·5
polyethylene	2·3

IV GUIDED WRITING

STAGE 1 *Paragraphing*

Divide this group of sentences into two paragraphs:

1. The capitance of a capacitor depends on three factors: the area of the plates, the distance between them, and the dielectric material which separates them. 2. Capacitance varies directly with the area of the plates but is inversely proportional to the distance between them. 3. In other words, the closer the plates, the greater the capacitance. 4. Dielectric materials are graded according to their dielectric constant. 5. The greater the dielectric constant, the greater the capacitance will be. 6. Capacitors can be classified according to the type of dielectric used. 7. General purpose capacitors have wax- or oil-impregnated paper as their dielectric. 8. Other types are named according to the dielectric used as mica, ceramic, and electrolytic. 9. A final type, which uses air as the dielectric, is the variable capacitor. 10. It is most commonly used as the tuning capacitor in radio receivers.

Now consider this question: What makes a group of sentences a paragraph? Here are some of the answers:

1. All the sentences are related in topic.
2. The sentences are logically linked. You have already studied some of these links. For example, generalization + qualification + reason. Some paragraphs are tightly structured; all the sentences have strong links like these. Other paragraphs are more loosely structured. The links between the sentences are not so strong.
3. There are grammar links between the sentences. For example, repeated nouns become pronouns.

Now here is the answer to the problem. You should have split the group after sentence 5. Sentences 1 to 5 are concerned with the three factors which affect the capacitance of a capacitor. That is the topic of the first paragraph. Sentences 6 to 10 are concerned with the classification of capacitors. That is the topic of the second paragraph.

There are logical links between the sentences in each paragraph. For example, sentence 3 restates part of sentence 2. There are also pronoun links between some of the sentences in each paragraph. Note how *variable capacitor* in sentence 9 becomes *it* in sentence 10.

STAGE 2 *Grouping sentences by topic*

Divide this group of sentences into three paragraphs. The topics are:

Paragraph 1 The disadvantages of continuous wave radar
Paragraph 2 The principle of pulse radar
Paragraph 3 The operation of a pulse radar system

1. A simple continuous wave radar system can detect a target.
2. It receives its own transmitted signal.
3. The transmitted signal is reflected from the target.
4. It cannot show how far away the target is.
5. It cannot distinguish one part of the transmitted signal from any other part.
6. Pulse radar provides information on the range of a target.
7. It transmits short pulses.
8. It does not transmit a continuous wave.
9. At the instant of transmission a timing device is set in motion.
10. The reflected signal is received.
11. The timing device is stopped.
12. The range can be calculated.
13. The transmitter generates a radio frequency.
14. The radio frequency may be 5 GHz.
15. The rf signal is fed in short bursts or pulses through a switch.
16. The switch opens briefly.
17. The switch allows the pulse to pass to the antenna.
18. A small part of the transmitted signal is fed to an attenuator.
19. The attenuated signal activates a trigger.
20. The trigger starts the horizontal sweep of the crt.
21. The horizontal axis of the crt becomes the time scale.
22. The time of transmission is marked by a vertical blip on this axis.
23. The antenna switch opens to the receiver.
24. The reflected pulse is received.
25. The received pulse is detected.
26. The detected pulse is fed to the Y plates of the crt.
27. A vertical blip appears on the screen at a position on the horizontal axis.
28. The position corresponds to the time of reception.
29. This can be compared with the time of transmission.
30. The target range can be calculated.

STAGE 3 *Paragraph building*

Now improve your paragraphs by linking some of the sentences together. Use the methods of linking sentences and ideas you have studied in earlier units. You may add words or phrases of your own.

STAGE 4 *Using a diagram to illustrate a passage*

The following diagram illustrates a pulse radar system. Insert references to the diagram in the completed passage.

EXAMPLE

The transmitter (1 on Figure 1) generates a radio frequency which may be 5 GHz.

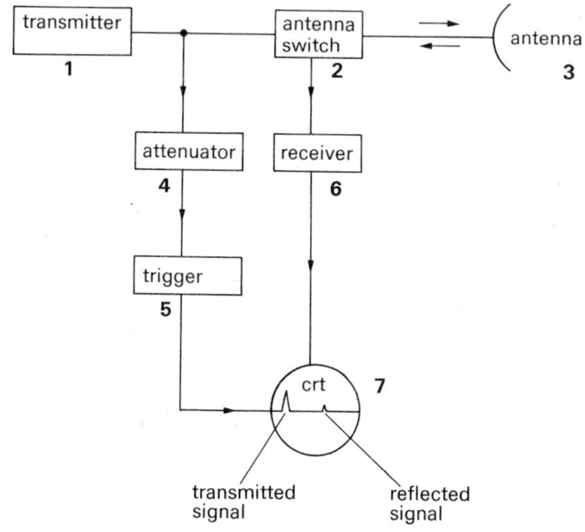

FIGURE 1

V READING AND SUMMARIZING

STAGE 1 *Reading for specific information*

Find the answers to these questions in the passage which follows. Work as quickly as you can. Try to ignore information which will not help you to answer the questions.

1. What part of the camera tube is scanned?
2. Why is the colour information lost?
3. What two types of information does the video-waveform carry?
4. What is the function of the sync pulses?

FROM CAMERA TO SCREEN

In this passage we will examine briefly how an object in front of a television camera becomes a picture on a television screen.

A television camera contains a lens system which is used to focus an image of the object on to the face of the camera tube. This tube contains a photo-cathode which emits electrons in response to light. The brighter the light from the image, the more electrons are emitted by the photo-cathode. In a black and white camera, the photo-cathode responds only to brightness, hence it is at this point that information on the colour of the image is lost. The electrons from the cathode are now made to strike a target electrode causing some of its atoms to become positively charged.

The target electrode is scanned by an electron beam. The beam sweeps the target electrode in a series of closely spaced lines. There are 405 or 625 of these lines depending on the system used. Figure 1 represents the scan path of the beam.

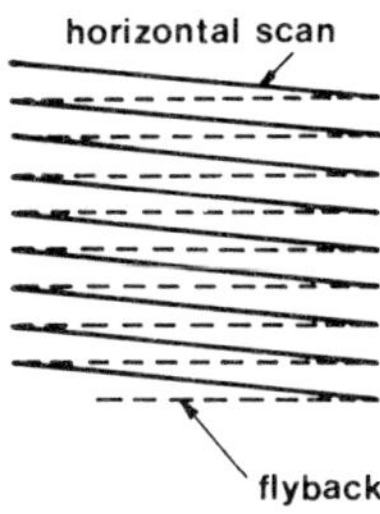

FIGURE 1

When the beam reaches the end of the top scan line, it is brought quickly back to the beginning of the next line which is slightly lower. This return is called flyback and is much quicker than a line scan.

The scanning beam loses electrons to the positively charged atoms on the target electrode and is thus changed or modulated. Its density is thus proportional to the light intensity of the original image. In this way the camera produces a continuous waveform which contains information on the brightness of the original image. This video waveform has information added to it, sync pulses, to synchronize the start of each scanning line and frame.

The video signal is transmitted and received in a similar fashion to sound transmissions. After detection and amplification it is fed to the cathode of the crt in the television receiver thus controlling the intensity of the electron beam. The sync pulses ensure that the beam in the crt is in exactly the same position as the beam in the television camera. The beam is made to move sideways and progressively downwards matching line by line the scanning of the television camera. As the electron beam strikes the television screen, the phosphor coating on the screen emits light. This light varies in whiteness according to the brightness of the original image. Because the line by line build up of the picture takes place so quickly, the eye sees only a complete picture of the object in front of the television camera.

STAGE 2 *Recognizing rephrasing*

Re-read lines 1 to 24. Then put these sentences below in the correct order with the help of the information contained in these lines. Sentence (a) is the first sentence.

(a) Light from an image is focused on to the camera tube photo-cathode.
(b) The target electrode is scanned by an electron beam in a series of closely spaced lines like a compressed zigzag.
(c) Sync pulses are added to the video waveform.
(d) The photo-cathode emits electrons according to the brightness of the light.
(e) The video signal is transmitted.
(f) The electrons from the photo-cathode strike the target electrode causing a pattern of positive charges to appear.
(g) The modulated beam is used to produce a video waveform carrying information on the brightness of the image.

STAGE 3 *Summarizing*

Write a paragraph summarizing lines 1 to 24 of the passage by linking the sentences in Stage 2.

Unit 6

I READING AND COMPREHENSION

PROCESS CONTROL SYSTEMS

Control systems provide a means of replacing human operators in many industrial processes. They are widely used to monitor and control pressure, temperature, motor speed, the flow of a liquid, or any other physical variable. They must be capable of fulfilling a number of functions. First, the physical variable to be controlled, such as the air temperature in a factory or the pressure of a hydraulic system, must be measured. Then its value must be compared with the desired value. Next, action has to be taken to reduce to zero the difference between the actual and desired value.

The basic components of a control system are an input transducer, an error sensor, a controller and an output transducer. The input transducer converts changes in the physical variable into electrical signals. Figure 1 shows one type of transducer which converts changes in pressure to frequency changes. Pressure changes move the diaphragm in or out, thus altering the position of the ferrite core in L_1 which forms part of a tuned circuit. This causes the frequency of the circuit to change, thus altering the output frequency of the oscillator. The output is then fed to an error sensor.

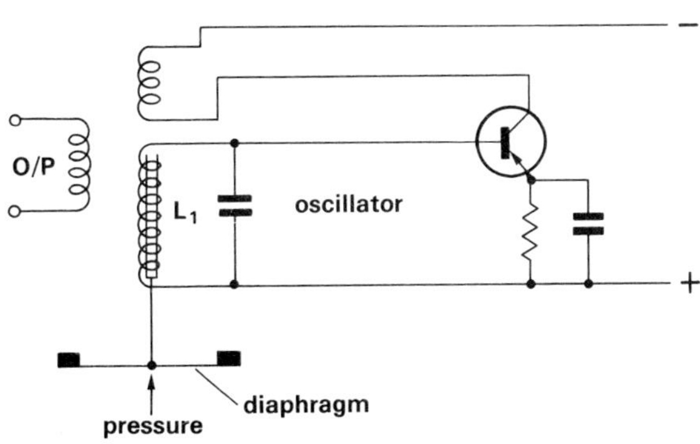

FIGURE 1

The error sensor measures the deviation between the actual and desired values for the variable. The controller receives the error sensor output and uses it to control the variable either directly or indirectly. A simple controller is an electromagnetic relay which uses a small signal to control a much larger signal such as a power supply output.

The output transducer converts the electrical output from the controller into whatever form of energy is required to change the physical variable. It may be a valve, a heater, a motor or any electrically operated piece of equipment. An example is a motor-operated valve which controls the flow of fluid in a pipeline.

Let us take as an example a process system for controlling the speed of a dc motor. The input transducer measures the speed and converts it into a voltage. The error sensor compares this voltage with the voltage across a speed-setting potentiometer. The error sensor output is fed to the controller which sends a signal to the power supply of the motor. This increases or reduces the supply of current to the motor, thus controlling its speed.

The operation of a process control system is summarized in Figure 2 which shows a closed-loop system. In such a system the results of the action of the controller are constantly fed back to it.

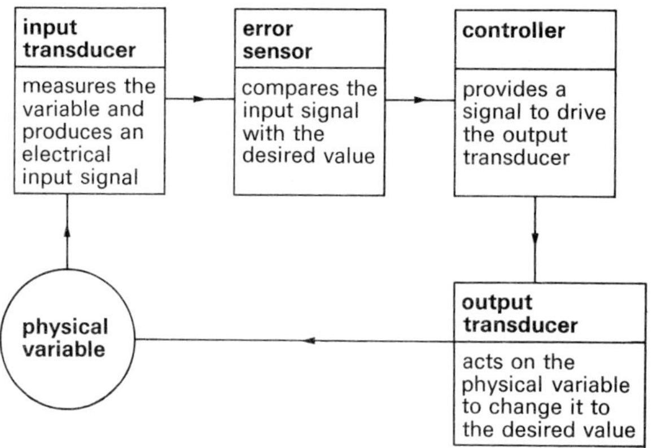

FIGURE 2

EXERCISE A *Meaning from context*

Select a word from the three alternatives given to replace the word in italics taken from the passage:

1. *monitor* (line 2)
   (a) warn
   (b) check
   (c) convert

2. *desired* (line 7)
   (a) actual
   (b) changed
   (c) required

3. *deviation* (line 17)
   (a) mistake
   (b) bias
   (c) difference

4. *converts* (line 22)
   (a) changes
   (b) controls
   (c) generates

EXERCISE B *Contextual reference*

What do the pronouns in italics in these sentences refer to?

1. *They* must be capable of fulfilling a number of functions. (line 4)
   (a) control systems
   (b) industrial processes
   (c) human operators
2. Then *its* value must be compared with the desired value. (line 6)
   (a) the pressure
   (b) the air temperature
   (c) the physical variable
3. *This* causes the frequency of the circuit to change, thus altering the output frequency of the oscillator. (line 14)
   (a) moving the diaphragm in or out
   (b) altering the position of the ferrite core
   (c) changing the pressure
4. *It* may be a valve, a heater, a motor, or any electrically operated piece of equipment. (line 23)
   (a) the output transducer
   (b) the electrical output
   (c) the physical variable
5. In *such a system* the results of the action of the controller are constantly fed back to it. (line 34)
   (a) a process control system
   (b) a closed-loop system
   (c) a system for controlling the speed of a dc motor

EXERCISE C *Finding out facts*

Answer these questions about the passage:

1. What must a process control system be capable of doing?
2. Compare an input transducer with an output transducer.
3. What is the function of an error sensor?
4. What is a closed-loop system?
5. How does a control system provide a means of replacing human operators?
6. Fill in the blanks in the following diagram to explain how the frequency-changing input transducer operates. Use the phrases given.

EXERCISE E *Allow/permit/let links*

Study this circuit and actions (i) and (ii) below:

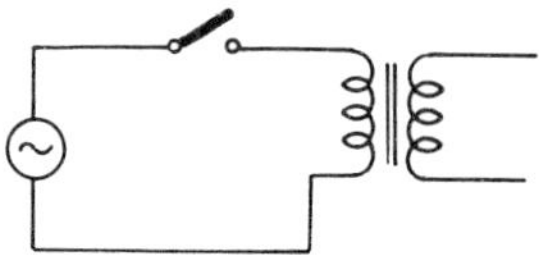

(i) the switch is closed
(ii) current flows through the transformer primary.
Action (i) *allows* action (ii) to happen. We can also link actions (i) and (ii) with *permit* and *let*.

EXAMPLES

1. The switch is closed ALLOWING current TO flow through the transformer primary.
2. The switch is closed PERMITTING current TO flow through the transformer primary.
3. The switch is closed LETTING current flow through the transformer primary.

We will represent an *allow/permit/let* link like this:

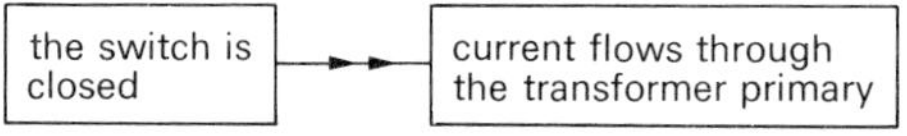
the switch is closed
current flows through the transformer primary

Study this circuit:

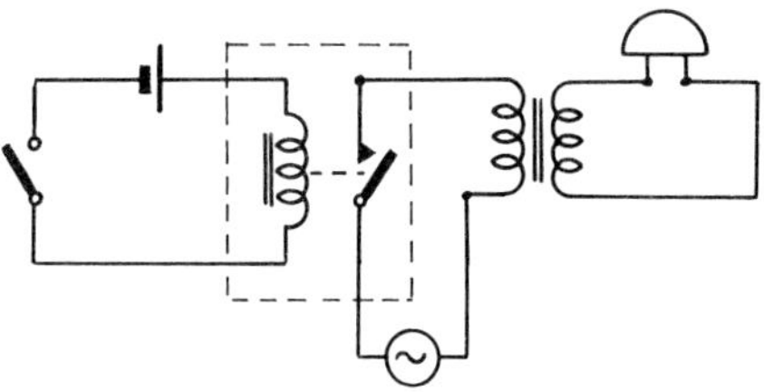

Using the circuit, put the events below in the correct sequence in the diagram. Event (b) is the first and has been entered for you.

(a) the supply current flows through the transformer primary
(b) the switch is closed
(c) the bell rings
(d) the armature is attracted to the core
(e) a voltage is induced in the secondary

(f) a magnetic field is set up round the core
(g) the secondary current flows through the bell
(h) the relay contacts are closed
(i) current flows through the relay coil

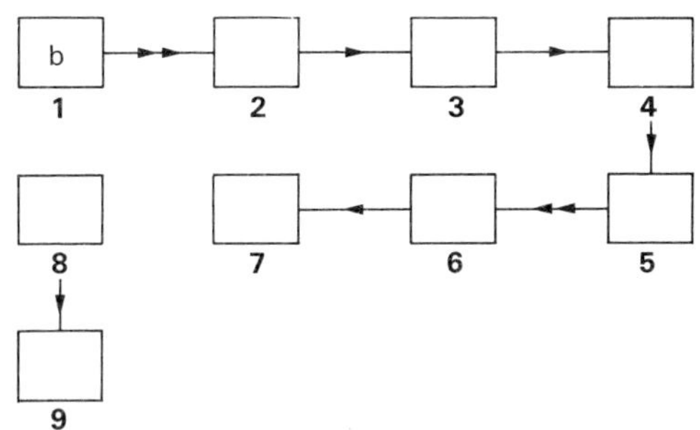

EXERCISE F *Describing cause and effect links in a circuit*

Now explain how the circuit operates by describing the links between each of the events in the completed diagram. Remember that a single arrow represents a *cause and effect* link and a double arrow an *allow/permit/let* link. You can also use these symbols in your note-taking.

EXERCISE G *Explaining the operation of a transducer*

Turn back to Exercise C, number 6, and write an explanation of how the frequency-changing input transducer operates using the diagram you completed.

EXERCISE H *Expressing possibility*

We use *can* or *may* to express possibility.

EXAMPLES

1. We MAY transform ac voltages.
2. We CANNOT transform dc voltages.

The previous sentences are personal. Most technical writing is impersonal. There are two ways to express possibility in an impersonal way:

We use *can* or *may* with the passive.

EXAMPLES

1. Ac voltages MAY BE transformed.
2. Dc voltages CANNOT BE transformed.

We use *it is possible/impossible*.

EXAMPLES

1. IT IS POSSIBLE to transform ac voltages.
2. IT IS IMPOSSIBLE to transform dc voltages.

Rewrite these sentences in two different ways to make them impersonal:

1. We can use the meter-bridge method for most experiments involving resistance.
2. We may classify most materials as conductors or insulators.
3. We cannot measure small currents accurately with an ammeter.
4. Often we can use a circuit breaker instead of a fuse.
5. You can heat non-conductors with a high frequency current.
6. Engineers cannot make an ideal transformer.
7. Often we can use a dc machine as a motor or as a generator.
8. We cannot operate dc machines on ac supplies.

EXERCISE I *Making classifying sentences*

Complete the spaces in this diagram using the list after it:

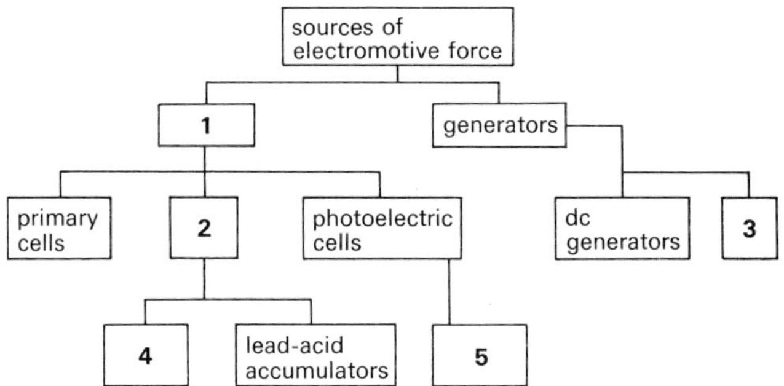

alternators, generators, sources of electromotive force, lead-acid accumulators, cells, solar cells, photoelectric cells, dc generators, secondary cells, nickel-cadmium cells.

This diagram classifies sources of electromotive force. Using it we can make classifying sentences:

EXAMPLES

1. Sources of electromotive force can be classified as/divided into cells and generators.
2. There are two main sources of electromotive force: cells and generators.

Now use the diagram to make classifying sentences about cells and generators.

EXERCISE J *Making classifying diagrams and sentences*

We often *support* a classifying sentence by giving an example.

EXAMPLE

1. There are two main sources of electromotive force: cells and generators. An example of a cell is the lead-acid accumulator. The alternator is an example of a generator.

Complete these diagrams from the lists given. Write as many classifying sentences as you can for each diagram. Add examples to support your classifying sentences.

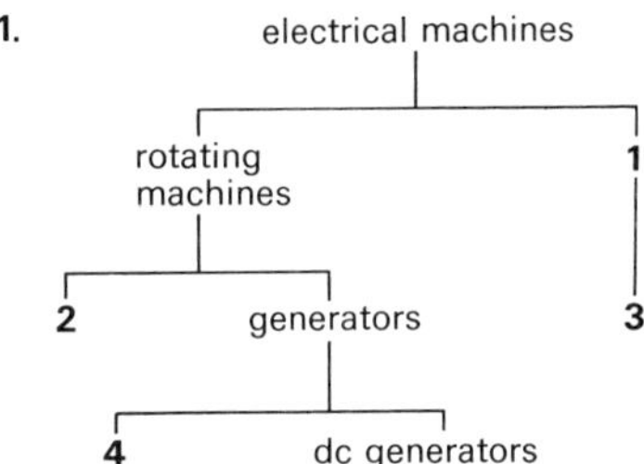

alternators, linear machines, electrical machines, motors, dc generators, linear motors, rotating machines, generators

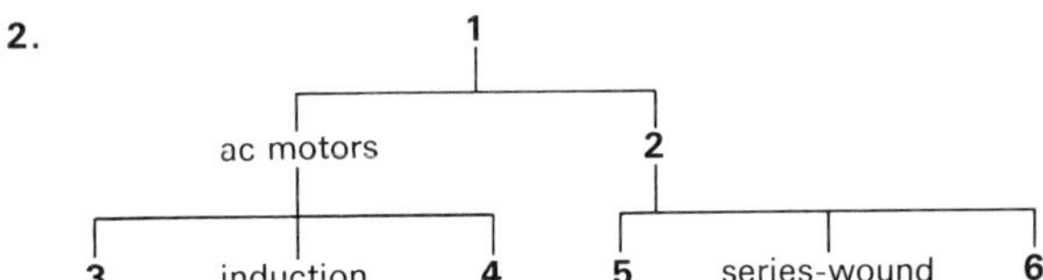

ac motors, electric motors, compound-wound, synchronous, variable-speed commutator, dc motors, series-wound, induction, shunt-wound

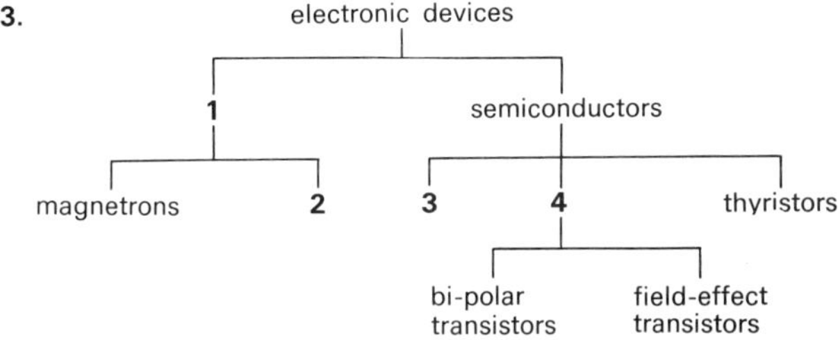

electronic devices, semiconductors, triodes, valves, thyristors, field-effect transistors, silicon diodes, transistors, bi-polar transistors, magnetrons.

III INFORMATION TRANSFER

EXERCISE K *Identifying resistor values*

In your practical work you will have to read the value of components. Often this is printed on the components using the abbreviations and symbols you have already learned. Resistors and some capacitors, however, use a colour code. The code is:

0	black	5	green
1	brown	6	blue
2	red	7	violet
3	orange	8	grey
4	yellow	9	white

On resistors these are normally coded as three bands. The third band is the multiplier. It indicates how many zeros to add. A fourth band indicates the tolerance according to this code:

gold	±	5%
silver	±	10%
no colour	±	20%
pink	±	high stability

EXAMPLE

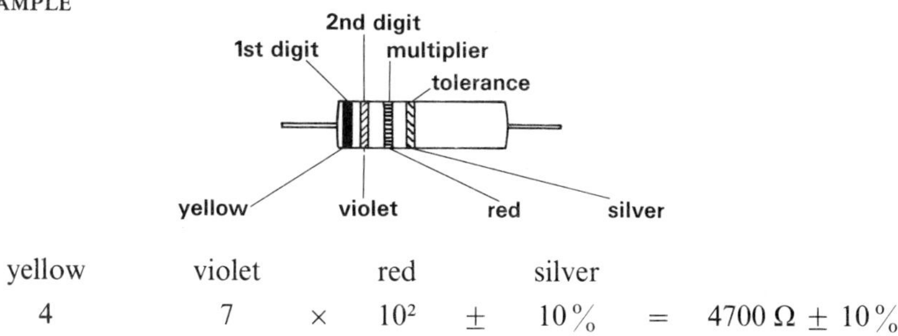

yellow		violet		red		silver		
4		7	×	10^2	±	10%	=	4700 Ω ± 10%

Now find the values and tolerances of resistors banded as follows:

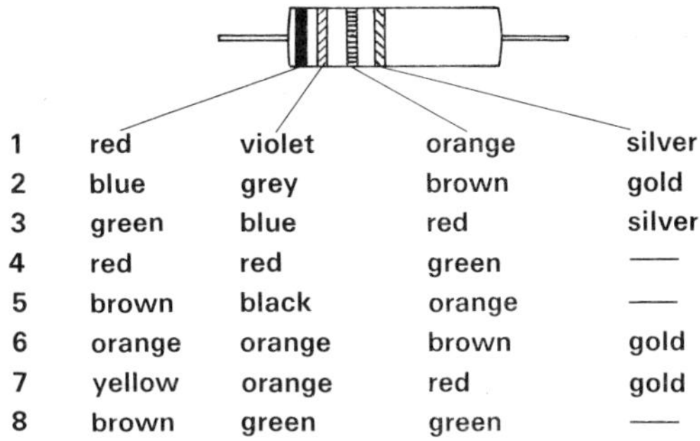

1	red	violet	orange	silver
2	blue	grey	brown	gold
3	green	blue	red	silver
4	red	red	green	—
5	brown	black	orange	—
6	orange	orange	brown	gold
7	yellow	orange	red	gold
8	brown	green	green	—

EXERCISE L *Describing how resistor values are determined*

Write a paragraph explaining how to determine the value of a colour-coded resistor.

IV GUIDED WRITING

STAGE 1 *Sentence building*

Join the following groups of sentences to make eleven longer sentences. You may add or omit words where you think it is necessary.

1. The fluorescent lamp consists of a glass tube.
   The tube is coated on the inside with a phosphor.
2. The tube is filled with mercury vapour.
   A small amount of argon is added to the mercury vapour.
3. A small tungsten filament is sealed into each end of the tube.
   The filament is coated with an electron emissive substance.
4. The filament electrodes heat.
   A stream of electrons flows between the filament electrodes.
5. These electrons collide with the electrons of the argon and mercury vapour in the tube.
   The two gases radiate ultraviolet light.
6. These rays bombard the phosphor coating.
   The phosphor coating is on the tube wall.
   The phosphor coating radiates visible light.
7. Many fluorescent tubes require a ballast choke and a starter switch.
   The ballast choke and the starter switch provide the initial ionization between the electrodes.
   The ionization starts the electron flow.
8. The supply is switched on.
   The starter switch is closed.
   The filaments heat up.
9. The starter switch opens.
   The filaments are hot.
   The ballast choke provides a high inductive voltage across the electrodes.
   The high inductive voltage starts the ionization.
10. Fluorescent lamp circuits also include a filter capacitor.
    The filter capacitor is fitted across the starter switch.
    The filter capacitor prevents radio interference.
11. A power factor correction capacitor is connected across the mains.
    The capacitor compensates for the inductance of the ballast choke.

STAGE 2 *Diagram labelling*

Label this fluorescent lamp circuit diagram with the following:

ballast choke, filter capacitor, mercury vapour and argon, starter switch, tungsten filaments, phosphor coating, power factor correction capacitor

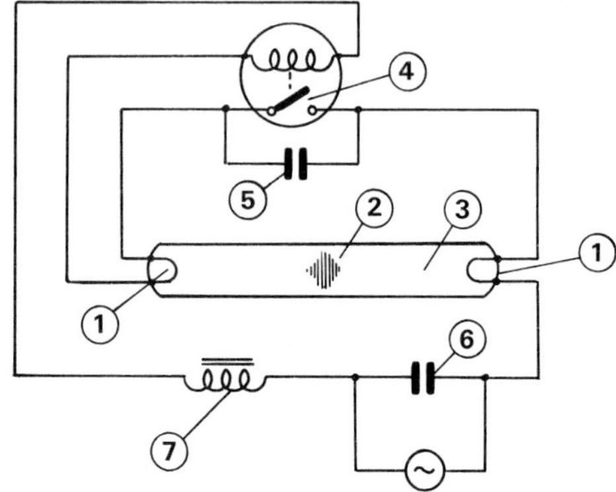

STAGE 3 *Paragraph building*

Group your completed sentences from Stage 1 into two paragraphs. Label the diagram *Figure 1* and insert a reference to it in the completed passage. Give the passage a suitable title.

V READING AND NOTE-TAKING

STAGE 1 *Reading for specific information*

Find the answers to these questions in the passage which follows. Work as quickly as you can. Try to ignore information which will not help you to answer the questions.

1. What is propagation?
2. How can radio waves travel great distances by sky waves?
3. Why is it best to use a frequency closest to the maximum usable frequency?

PROPAGATION

A signal from a transmitter may be propagated in three ways: by ground waves, by space waves and by sky waves. Ground waves travel round the surface of the earth for short distances. As they travel, they lose energy. This loss of power, or attenuation, depends on the nature of the surface. Attenuation also varies with the frequency of the signal: the higher the frequency, the greater the ground wave attenuation. At frequencies above 20 MHz the range is reduced to line of sight.

Propagation by space waves applies mainly to very high frequencies. Part of the transmitted signal travels in a direct line from transmitting antenna to receiving antenna. Partly the signal is reflected from the ground. The higher the frequency, the greater the possible ground wave reflection. The range of space wave propagation is restricted to approximately twice the direct optical path.

The range covered by ground waves and space waves is limited. Greater distances can be achieved using sky waves. Sky wave propagation depends on the ionosphere.

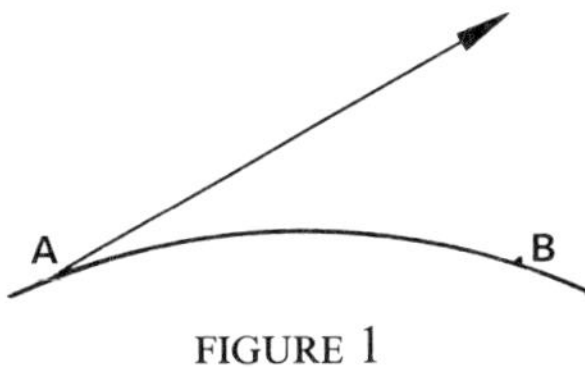

FIGURE 1

A signal transmitted from point A would not be received at B because of the curvature of the earth if it were not for the ionosphere. This consists of a number of layers of ionized gas in the upper atmosphere. If a transmission is directed towards these layers, it will be reflected back to earth as shown in Figure 2.

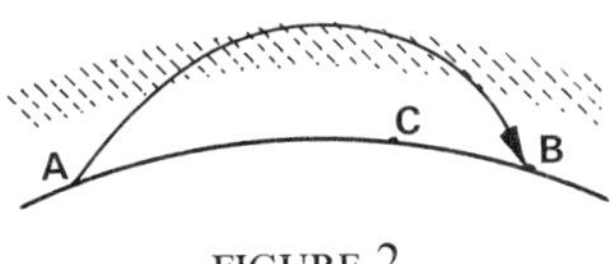

FIGURE 2

The wave may then be reflected back from the earth to the ionosphere. Indeed it may be carried right round the earth by successive reflections although it will lose power both in the earth and in the ionosphere at each bounce. A receiver at point C, which is outside ground wave range yet closer than B, will not receive the transmission.

The bending effect of the ionosphere depends on the frequency of the signal and the angle of radiation. The higher the frequency, the less the bending. At a certain frequency, signals will pass straight through the layers and be lost in space. The smaller the angle of radiation, the greater the distance which can be covered in one reflection.

At any time there is a maximum usable frequency for transmissions from a given site over a particular path. This frequency depends on the state of the ionosphere which varies according to many factors including the time of day and the season of the year. The lower the frequency of a transmission, the greater the number of reflections needed to cover the required distance and hence the weaker the signal will be. For this reason, it is best to use a frequency as high as possible without exceeding the maximum usable frequency as this will cover the required distance with the smallest number of reflections and hence the least attenuation.

STAGE 2 *Comprehension*

Now read the passage again carefully. Find the answers to these questions:

1. List three types of propagation.
2. How do ground waves travel?
3. What is attenuation?
4. Name two factors which affect the attenuation of ground waves.
5. What frequencies are propagated by space waves?
6. Name two ways in which space waves travel.
7. What range have space waves?
8. What controls sky wave propagation?
9. What is the ionosphere?
10. How do sky waves cover great distances?
11. Name two factors which determine the bending effect of the ionosphere.
12. What is the maximum usable frequency?

Reconsider your answers to Stage 1. Have they changed with a more careful reading?

STAGE 3 *Note-taking*

Complete this framework of notes using your answers to Stages 1 and 2. The symbol ∼ here means *depends on* and the symbol ∵ means *because*.

Propagation
Types: . . . . . .
Ground waves travel . . . . . .
Attenuation = ...
Ground wave attenuation ∼ (i) . . . . . .
(ii) . . . . . .
Space waves used for . . . . . .
They travel (i) . . . . . .
(ii) . . . . . .
Their range is . . . . . .
Sky wave propagation ∼ . . . . . .
Ionosphere = ...
Sky waves travel great distances by . . . . . .
Ionosphere bending effect ∼ 1. . . . . . .
2. . . . . . .
Maximum usable frequency = ...
Maximum usable frequency ∼ . . . . . .
A frequency close to it should be used ∵ . . . . . .

Unit 7

I READING AND COMPREHENSION

SEMICONDUCTOR DIODES

If two crystals of a semiconductor material, one of p-type and one of n-type, are joined together, a pn junction is formed. This junction can be used as a rectifier and is known as a pn junction diode.

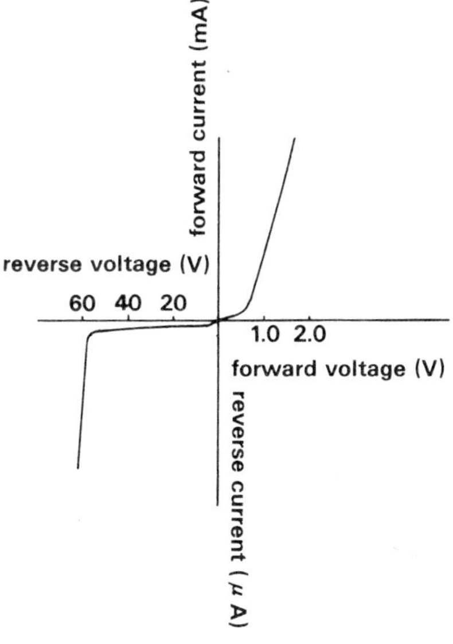

FIGURE 1

Figure 1 illustrates what happens when a voltage is applied across a silicon pn junction diode. The first quadrant of the graph shows the characteristics of the diode when the source is connected with the positive to the p-side of the junction and the negative to the n-side. In other words, the diode is forward biased. With forward bias, the current at first increases slowly. When the applied voltage reaches about 600 mV, the current rises rapidly. The diode is then a good conductor. The current will continue to rise with increased voltage but eventually a point will be reached where the diode is destroyed by heat.

The third quadrant shows the characteristics when the source is connected with the positive to the n-side and the negative to the p-side. When the diode is reverse biased, there is almost no current flow. The junction is therefore a good rectifier: it conducts well in one direction and almost not at all in the other. However there is a small reverse leakage current. This leakage current remains substantially constant until what is known as breakdown voltage (Vb) is reached. At this point there is a sharp increase in the reverse current. This sudden increase in current is called the Zener effect.

Normal diodes are never operated in the breakdown region but Zener diodes are designed to make use of the breakdown phenomenon. Because any slight increase in voltage beyond the breakdown point causes a large increase in current, Zener diodes are often used as a kind of overspill to protect sensitive circuits from fluctuations in the power supply.

EXERCISE A *Meaning from context*

Select a word from the three alternatives given which is most similar in meaning to the word in italics as it is used in the passage:

1. *characteristics* (line 5)
   (a) typical behaviour
   (b) voltage figures
   (c) graph
2. *substantially* (line 18)
   (a) almost
   (b) greatly
   (c) hardly
3. *sharp* (line 19)
   (a) slight
   (b) steep
   (c) cutting
4. *phenomenon* (line 22)
   (a) voltage
   (b) effect
   (c) result
5. *fluctuations* (line 25)
   (a) rises and falls
   (b) increases
   (c) failures

EXERCISE B *Recognizing rephrasing*

Find a sentence in the passage which is similar in meaning to each of these sentences:

1. The positive of the source is connected to the p-side of the diode and the negative to the n-side.
2. When a forward voltage is applied across the diode, there is, at first, only a slow rise in current.
3. The diode allows current to flow freely.
4. If a reverse voltage is applied to the diode, it conducts badly.
5. There is almost no change in leakage current until the reverse voltage reaches breakdown point.

EXERCISE C *Describing diode characteristics*

Complete this description of the current–voltage characteristics of a silicon diode. Use the passage and Figure 1 to help you.

> At first, when a forward voltage is applied, ... When the forward voltage has reached about 600 mV, ... If the forward voltage is further increased, ... only a very small leakage current flows. When the breakdown voltage is reached, ... After the breakdown point, any further increase in reverse voltage causes . . . . . .

EXERCISE D *Checking facts and ideas*

Decide if these statements are true or false. Quote from the passage to support your decisions.

1. The first quadrant of the graph shows the characteristics of the diode in forward bias.
2. For forward voltages over 600 mV, the diode conducts well.
3. When the source is connected with the negative to the n-side and the positive to the p-side, the diode is reverse biased.
4. When a reverse voltage is first applied, a diode conducts badly.
5. Zener diodes are never used beyond breakdown point.

II USE OF LANGUAGE

EXERCISE E *Time clauses*

Time clauses relate two actions in time. In this section we will study clauses relating:

1. Simultaneous actions

EXAMPLE

> As the voltage increases, the current rises.

2. Actions in immediate succession

EXAMPLE

> When the switch is pressed, the light goes on.

3. An action and its limit

EXAMPLE

> The current increases until the diode is destroyed by heat.

1. Simultaneous actions

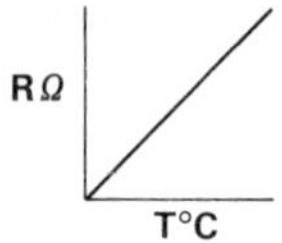

Study this graph. It represents two actions which happen at the same time, i.e. two simultaneous actions.

Action (i) the temperature rises
Action (ii) the resistance rises

We can link two simultaneous actions using *as*.

EXAMPLE

AS the temperature rises, the resistance rises.

We will represent simultaneous actions like this:

action (i)
action (ii)

2. Actions in immediate succession

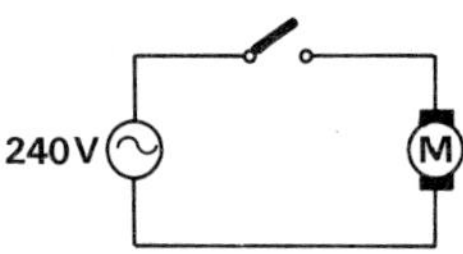

Study this circuit and note how action (i) is followed immediately by action (ii).

Action (i) the switch is closed
Action (ii) the motor starts

We can link actions in immediate succession using *when* or *as soon as*.

EXAMPLE

WHEN the switch is closed, the motor starts.

We will represent actions in immediate succession like this:

action (i)	action (ii)

3. Action and limit

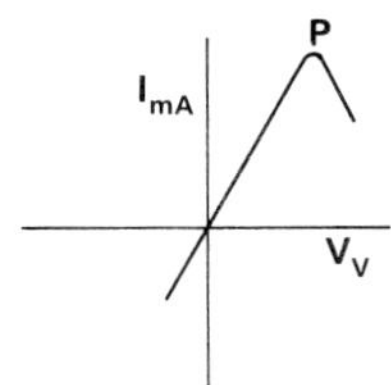

This graph shows an action and its limit.

Action the current rises steadily
Limit point P is reached

We can link an action and its limit using *until.*

EXAMPLE

The current rises steadily UNTIL point P is reached.

We will represent this relationship like this:

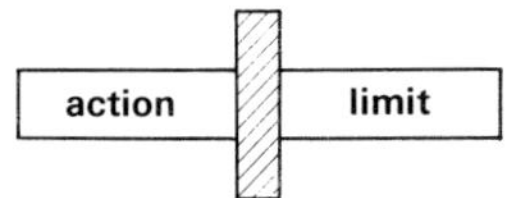

You have already studied ways to relate actions in sequence in Unit 5.

EXAMPLE

AFTER the signal has been detected, it is amplified.

Remember that we represent actions in sequence like this:

Now link these pairs of actions using time clauses. The diagrams indicate the relationship between each pair.

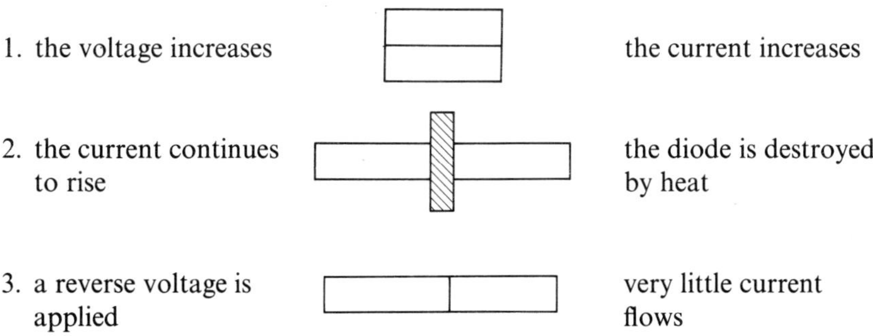

1. the voltage increases
the current increases
2. the current continues to rise
the diode is destroyed by heat
3. a reverse voltage is applied
very little current flows

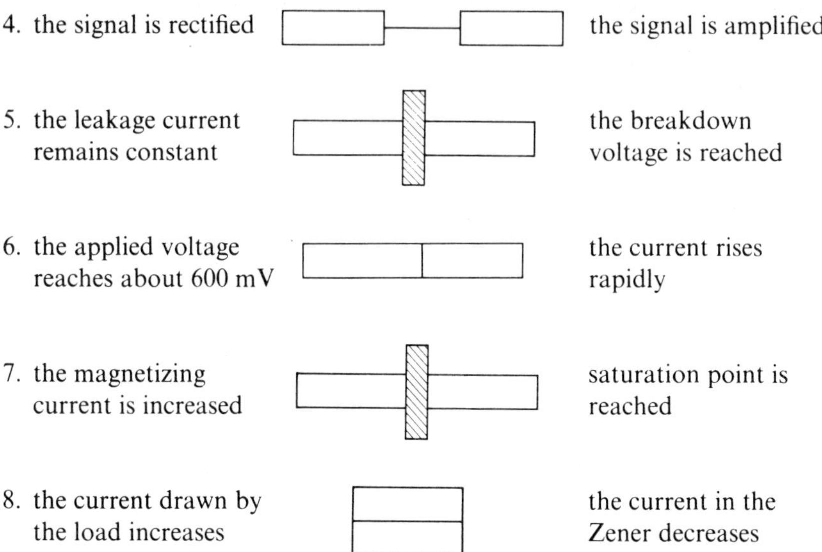

4. the signal is rectified
the signal is amplified
5. the leakage current remains constant
the breakdown voltage is reached
6. the applied voltage reaches about 600 mV
the current rises rapidly
7. the magnetizing current is increased
saturation point is reached
8. the current drawn by the load increases
the current in the Zener decreases

EXERCISE F *Describing the operation of a moving-coil meter*

The actions below occur in the operation of a moving-coil meter. Link them as indicated in the diagram to make a description of the operation of the moving-coil meter. The reading passage for Unit 5, page 52, will also help you.

1. The meter is inserted in a live circuit.
2. Current flows through the control springs to the coil.
3. A magnetic field is set up round the coil.
4. The field reacts with the radial magnetic field in the annular gap.
5. A torque is produced.
6. The torque rotates the coil.
7. The coil rotates.
8. The springs tighten.
9. The coil continues to rotate.
10. The deflecting force of the coil balances the controlling force of the springs.
11. The coil is brought to rest with the pointer showing the magnitude of the current on the scale.

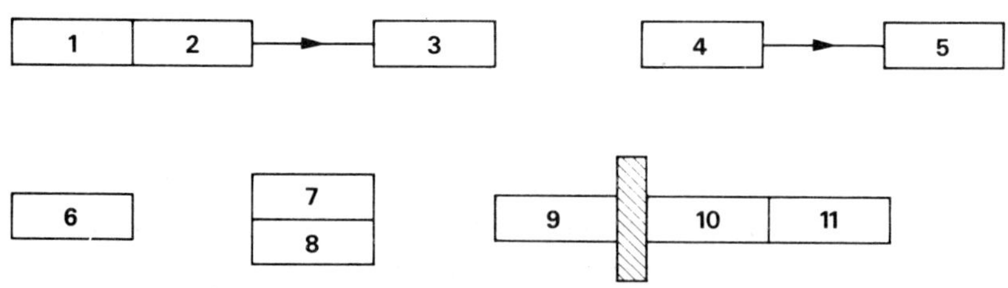

EXERCISE G *Describing the operation of a burglar alarm*

Study this circuit of a burglar alarm. The relay is shown in its unenergized state.

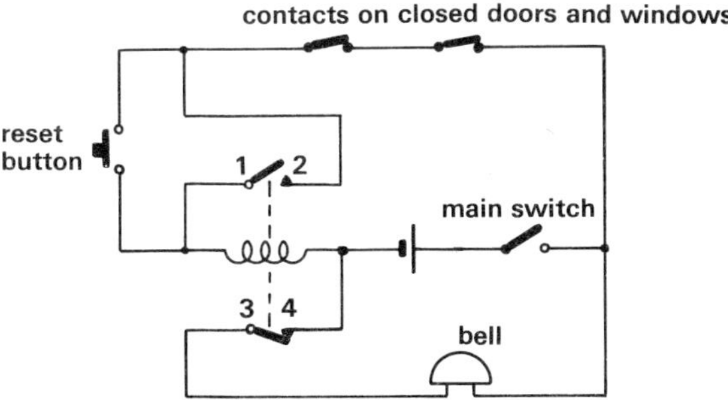

Now describe the operation of the alarm. Start your description like this:

> The relay is set by closing the main switch and pressing the reset button. This allows current from the battery ......

EXERCISE H *Generalizations*

In Unit 6 you classified sources of electromotive force. Here is part of the diagram you made. Note that it has three levels.

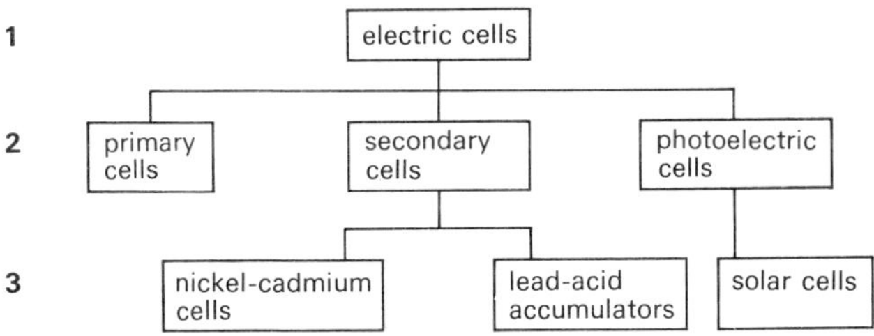

Now study these sentences. There is one about each level of the diagram.

1. Electric cells produce current from chemical or light energy.
2. Photoelectric cells change light energy into electric energy.
3. Solar cells convert sunlight into electric energy.

Each sentence is a generalization. That is, it is a statement about a whole class of items. We can write a generalization in three ways if the item is something that can be counted, e.g. a resistor, a motor.

EXAMPLES

1. Electric cells produce current from chemical or light energy.
2. The electric cell produces current from chemical or light energy.
3. An electric cell produces current from chemical or light energy.

III INFORMATION TRANSFER

EXERCISE K *Reading transistor characteristics*

The chart below shows the characteristics of a number of transistors manufactured by Mullard Ltd.

1	2	3	4	5	6	7	8	9
Type	Polarity	P_{tot} W	at T_{mb} °C	I_{CM} A	$I_{C\,max}$ $A^{(d.c.)}$	BV_{CBO} V	BV_{CEO} V	BV_{EBO} V
BD124	N	15	60	4	2	70	45	6
BD131/3	N	11	60	6	3	70/90	45/60	6
BD132	P	11	60	6	3	45	45	4
BD135/7/9	N	6·5	60	1·5	0·5	45/60/100	45/60/80	5
BD136/8/40	P	6·5	60	1·5	0·5	45/60/100	45/60/80	5

	10	11	12	13	14	15	16	17
Type	h_{FE}	at V_{CE} V	I_C A	V_{CE} (sat) V	at I_C A	I_B A	f_T MHz	at I_C A
BD124	25 min	5	2	0·50 typ	2	0·2	120 typ	0·25
BD131/3	20 min	1	2	0·9 max	2	0·2	60 min	0·25
BD132	20 min	1	2	0·9 max	2	0·2	60 min	0·25
BD135/7/9	25 min	2	0·5	0·5 max	0·5	0·05	250 typ	0·05
BD136/8/40	25 min	2	0·5	0·5 max	0·5	0·05	75 typ	0·05

Study this description of the characteristics of one of these transistors and make yourself familiar with the English meaning of each of the abbreviations used in the chart. The characteristics have been numbered in both chart and description to help you.

> The BD124 (1) is a silicon NPN (2) transistor manufactured by Mullard. It dissipates a maximum power of 15 watts (3) at a mounting base temperature of 60°C (4). The peak collector current it can pass is 4 amps (5). The maximum permitted dc current flowing out of the collector terminal is 2 amps (6). The collector-base breakdown voltage, with the emitter disconnected, is 70 volts (7). The collector-emitter junction would break down at 45 volts (8). The voltage at which the emitter-base junction would

break down is 6 volts (9). None of these breakdown voltages should be exceeded.

The dc current amplification factor is at least 25 (10) when measured at a collector-emitter voltage of 5 volts (11) and a collector current of 2 amps (12).

The collector-emitter saturation voltage is typically 0·50 volts (13). The collector current at saturation voltage is 2 amps (14) and the base current 0·2 amps (15). These characteristics are important in switching circuits. They represent the conditions under which the transistor is *on*.

The frequency at which the current gain would be reduced to 1 is typically 120 MHz (16). The collector current at this frequency would be 0·25 amps (17).

EXERCISE L *Describing transistor characteristics*

Now complete this description of the BD132:

The BD132 is a silicon (a). . . . . . transistor. It dissipates (b). . . . . . at a mounting base temperature of 60°C. The peak collector current is (c). . . . . . The maximum dc (d). . . . . . is 3 amps. The breakdown voltages for the collector-base, (e). . . . . . and emitter-base junctions are (f). . . . . ., 45 V, and (g). . . . . . respectively.

Dc current gain is at least (h). . . . . . when measured at a collector-emitter voltage of (i). . . . . . and a (j). . . . . . of 2 amps.

A collector-emitter voltage drop of a maximum of 0·9 volts exists when a (k). . . . . . of 2 amps and a base current of (l). . . . . . amps flow. These are the saturation conditions for this transistor.

The frequency at which the current gain would be reduced to 1 is (m). . . . . . The collector current at this frequency would be (n). . . . . .

IV GUIDED WRITING

STAGE 1 *Writing explanations 1*

A good explanation allows the reader to link his knowledge with that of the writer. A bad explanation either over-estimates the reader's knowledge with the result that he cannot understand it, or under-estimates the reader's knowledge so that he is bored.

Study the following explanations. They all try to explain why conductors are coated with plastic.

1. Conductors are coated with plastic because plastic is an insulator.

Explanation 1 is effective if the reader knows what an insulator is.

2. Conductors are coated with plastic because plastic is an insulator. An insulator does not readily release electrons.

Explanation 2 is effective if the reader knows that current is carried by electrons.

3. Conductors are coated with plastic because plastic is an insulator. An insulator does not readily release electrons. Free electrons carry current and thus no current can pass through the plastic.

Explanation 3 is effective for the reader who does not know what an insulator is nor how current is carried.

Explanations often involve answering *how* and *why* questions.

EXAMPLES

1. Copper is a good conductor (*why?*) BECAUSE it readily releases electrons.
2. Use a heat shunt when soldering sensitive components (*why?*) SO THAT they are not damaged by heat.
3. The current flowing through a resistor can be calculated (*how?*) BY DIVIDING the voltage by the resistance.
4. The rf section of a receiver is sometimes screened (*why?*) TO PREVENT interference from other parts of the receiver.

Now answer the *why?* and *how?* questions following each of these statements. Use the information given below.

1. Soldering wire contains flux (*why?*) to . . . . .
2. When a current flows through the filament of a lamp, it gives off light (*why?*) because . . . . . .
3. The value of a resistor can be calculated from the colour bands on the body (*how?*) by . . . . . .
4. Manganin wire is used for the elements of an electric wire (*why?*) because of . . . . . .
5. Sensitive equipment is protected by fuses (*why?*) so that . . . . . .
6. Lamps may contain rare gases (*why?*) to . . . . . .
7. Curved pole shoes are fitted to meter magnets (*why?*) so that . . . . . .
8. When a relay is energized, sets of contacts are pushed together or apart (*how?*) by means of . . . . . .

(a) The pole shoes help form a radial magnetic field.
(b) The filament becomes incandescent.
(c) The equipment is not damaged by excess current.
(d) The gases prevent the filament burning up.
(e) The flux prevents the surfaces being joined from oxidizing.
(f) A relay contains a moving armature which controls the contacts.

(g) Manganin has a higher resistance than most metals.
(h) The colour code is used to determine the value of a resistor.

STAGE 2 *Writing explanations 2*

With the help of a suitable textbook, write your own explanation of the operation of one of the following:

1. a relay
2. a microphone (any type)
3. a transformer
4. a dc motor

V READING AND SUMMARIZING

STAGE 1 *Reading for specific information*

Find all the answers to these questions in the passage which follows. Work as quickly as you can. Try to ignore information which will not help you to answer the questions.

1. What is modulation?
2. Which three quantities of a wave can be modulated?
3. Why is frequency modulation better than amplitude modulation?

MODULATION

We can only communicate information by radio waves by changing the wave in some way. This change is known as modulation. The simplest form of modulation is to turn the wave on and off. This method was used in the early days of radio for telegraphic signals. The wave was stopped and started to represent the dots and dashes of the Morse code by means of a telegraph key.

Speech and music produce audio frequencies which cannot be transmitted directly. But they can be used to modulate radio waves. The modulated radio wave is then transmitted. When it is received, the wave is demodulated and the original audio-frequency signal is recovered. The high frequency radio wave acts only to carry the audio-frequency signal and is called the carrier wave. The audio-frequency signal is termed the modulating signal.

A wave has three quantities: amplitude, frequency and phase. Any of these quantities can be modulated. The two commonest methods of modulation are amplitude modulation, am, and frequency modulation, fm.

In amplitude modulation, the amplitude of the carrier wave is changed according to the amplitude of the modulating signal. The frequency of the carrier is kept constant. Figure 1 represents part of an audio-frequency signal, which might be generated by a microphone. Figure 2 represents a radio wave of much higher frequency. Figure 3 shows the same radio frequency wave after it has been modulated by the audio-frequency signal in Figure 1.

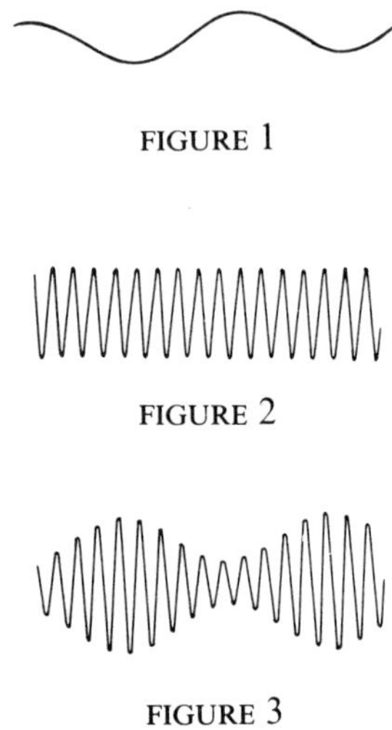

FIGURE 1

FIGURE 2

FIGURE 3

In frequency modulation, the amplitude of the carrier wave is kept constant, but the frequency is varied in proportion to the amplitude of the modulating signal. Frequency modulation has several advantages over amplitude modulation. The most notable is that reception is less likely to be disturbed. This is because atmospheric disturbances and 'noise' generated in the receiver itself result in a change in the amplitude of the received signal. However, changes in only the frequency would distort the modulated information.

In fm sound broadcasting, the limit of frequency deviation is usually 75 kHz above and below the frequency of the unmodulated carrier wave. In other words, fm broadcasts require a considerable bandwidth either side of the carrier frequency. This is one reason why fm stations broadcast in the vhf band (30–300 MHz) where stations can be spaced more than several hundred kilohertz apart unlike the medium frequency bands where spacings of only 9 to 10 kHz are common.

STAGE 2 *Recognizing rephrasing*

Now read the whole passage carefully. Each of these sentences summarizes part of the passage. Identify the lines summarized:

1. In fm the frequency of the carrier wave is modulated according to the amplitude of the modulating signal. (lines . . . . . .)

2. Audio frequencies cannot be transmitted. (lines . . . . . .)
3. The amplitude, frequency and phase of a wave can be modulated. (lines . . . . . .)
4. Fm broadcasts are in the vhf band partly because fm stations require greater spacing. (lines . . . . . .)
5. The carrier wave is demodulated by the receiver and the audio-frequency signal recovered. (lines . . . . . .)
6. No information can be communicated by radio waves without modulating them. (lines . . . . . .)
7. In am the amplitude of the carrier wave is modulated according to the amplitude of the modulating signal. (lines . . . . . .)
8. Stopping and starting the wave is the simplest method of modulation (lines . . . . . .)
9. Fm is better than am because there is less interference. (lines . . . . . .)
10. Audio frequencies can be used to modulate high frequency radio waves which can then act as carriers of the audio-frequency signal. (lines . . . . . .)

STAGE 3 *Summarizing*

Put the sentences in Stage 2 in the correct order and use them to make a paragraph summarizing the passage. You may add words of your own to make a good paragraph. Make sure no information is repeated unnecessarily.

Unit 8

I READING AND COMPREHENSION

LOGIC GATES

Logic gates are electronic switching devices. Figure 1 represents in simple terms the function of one type of logic gate, the OR gate.

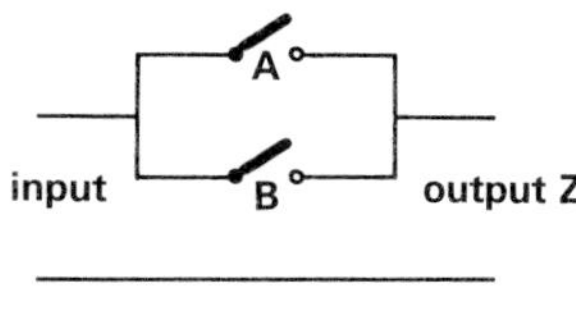

FIGURE 1

If switch A is closed, the output Z will equal the input. Similarly if B is closed, or if both A and B are closed, the output and input will be equal. Any of these three conditions will permit an output Z to flow.

Logic gates contain semiconductors, not mechanical switches, which can be opened and closed. But they have only two levels of input and output: a high level and a low level. These correspond to the closed and open states of the switches in Figure 1. The high level is represented by 1 and the low level by 0. All information in digital systems is transmitted in terms of these two levels.

We can make a table to represent the output value of an OR gate for all possible combinations of inputs. Such a table is called a truth table. A truth table can be made for any logic gate.

input		output
A	B	Z
0	0	0
1	0	1
0	1	1
1	1	1

FIGURE 2

We can summarize this table by the formula, Z = A + B where the symbol + stands for OR.

Other common digital devices are AND, NOR and NAND gates, and inverters. AND gates will have an output of 1 only if 1 is present on all inputs. An inverter is a device which inverts its input. Thus an input of 0 will have an output of 1 and vice-versa. Complex circuits are made by combining these basic devices. Their circuit symbols are as follows:

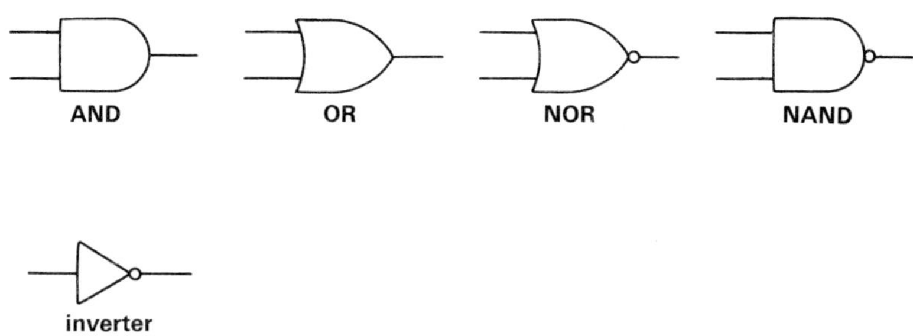

FIGURE 3

Let us now consider an example of the use of logic gates to control an industrial process. Suppose a motor controlling the flow of aluminium blanks to a hydraulic press is to be switched on only under the following conditions:

1. the switch is on
2. the supply voltage is correct
3. there is a supply of aluminium blanks in the feed-hopper
4. the pressure in the hydraulic system of the press is correct.

Information on these four conditions will be fed into an AND gate as *all* four must be satisfied for the motor to run. The output from the AND gate will be a logic level which is fed into the store input of the memory unit to provide a continuous signal to operate the motor.

The motor must stop if any one of the following conditions arises:

1. the switch is off
2. the supply voltage rises too high
3. the hopper is empty
4. the pressure in the hydraulic system drops.

Information of these conditions will be fed into an OR gate as the presence of *any* one must result in the motor being stopped.

An input of 1 from the OR gate to the memory reset input will remove the continuous output and hence stop the motor. The complete system will look like this:

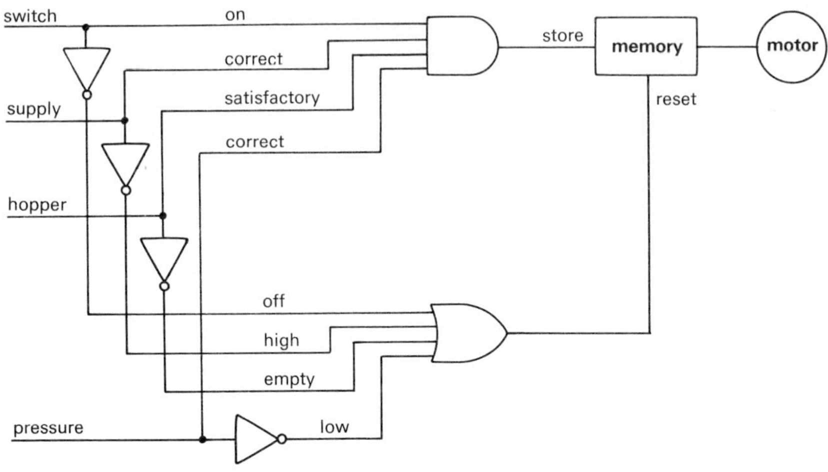

FIGURE 4

EXERCISE A *Relationships between statements*

Substitute expressions of similar meaning for the following words in the passage to show clearly the relationship between the statements they link:

1. similarly (line 3)
2. but (line 7)
3. thus (line 18)
4. as (line 37)
5. hence (line 40)

EXERCISE B *Finding out facts*

Answer these questions with reference to the passage:

1. In what way are logic gates like mechanical switches?
2. This circuit represents the function of an AND gate:

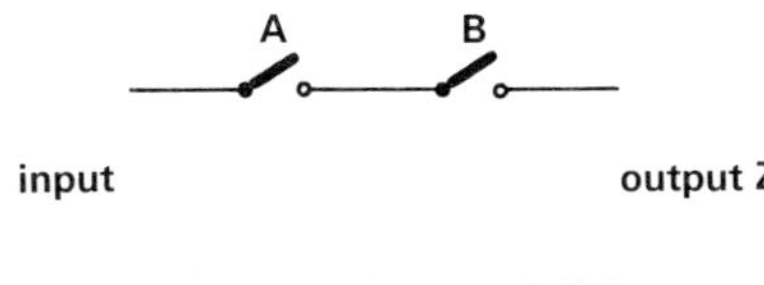

Complete this truth table for an AND gate:

A	B	Z
0	0	0

3. What will be the output of this circuit for an input of 1 at B and 0 at A and C?

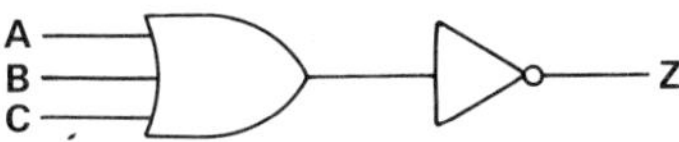

4. Explain how the hopper becoming empty will stop the feed motor.

EXERCISE C *Making definitions*

Use information from the passage to make definitions of the items below:

EXAMPLE

a logic gate
A logic gate is an electronic switching device which responds to two levels of input: a high level represented by 1 and a low level represented by 0.

1. a truth table
2. an inverter
3. an OR gate
4. an AND gate

II USE OF LANGUAGE

EXERCISE D *Making predictions*

We make predictions when we describe what the consequences of an action will be. Predictions link two actions in time. Both actions are in the future but we use the future tense for only the probable consequence. The other action is put in the present tense.

EXAMPLES

1. If the switch is pressed, THE BELL WILL RING.
2. If the current rises to 170% normal, THE FUSE WILL BLOW.

Now predict the consequences of each of these actions. The diagrams will help you with actions 5 to 8.

1. Action: If a current of 3A is passed across a fuse rated at 500 mA, ...
2. Action: If a current-carrying conductor is placed in a magnetic field, ...
3. Action: If too large a current flows through a semiconductor diode, ...
4. Action: If a screwdriver is placed across the terminals of a charged electrolytic capacitor, ...

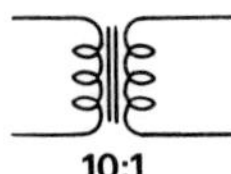

5. Action: If 120 V ac is applied across the transformer primary, ...

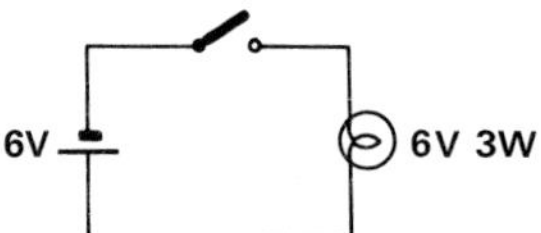

6. Action: If the switch is closed, ...

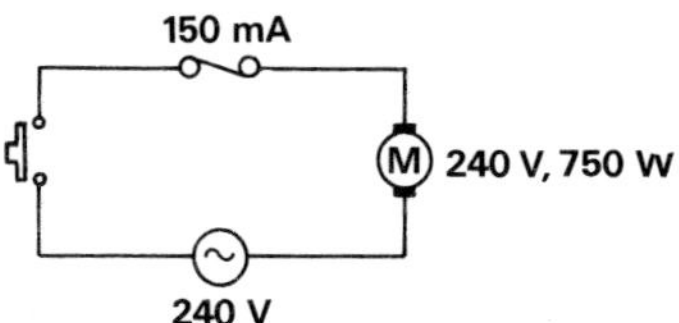

7. Action: If the switch is pressed, ...

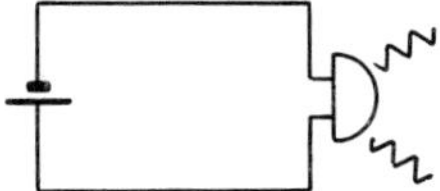

8. Action: If the circuit is broken, ...

EXERCISE E *Fault finding 1: probability*

Study this circuit:

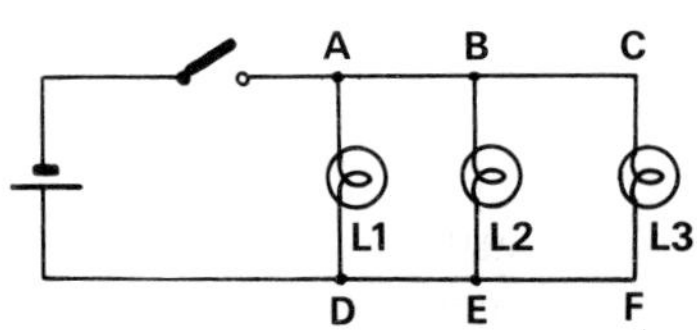

This circuit can have a number of faults. One fault and its possible causes are listed here:

FAULT	POSSIBLE CAUSES
No lamps light	(a) open circuit before A or D
	(b) flat battery
	(c) broken filaments in L_1, L_2 and L_3

We can grade these possible causes according to how probable they are. For example, causes (a) and (b) are both fairly likely. We can say:

1. This fault MAY be due to an open circuit before A or D.
2. This fault MAY be caused by a flat battery.

Cause (c) is much less likely. We can say:

3. This fault MIGHT be due to broken filaments in L_1, L_2 and L_3.

We can express probability using a verb from this scale:

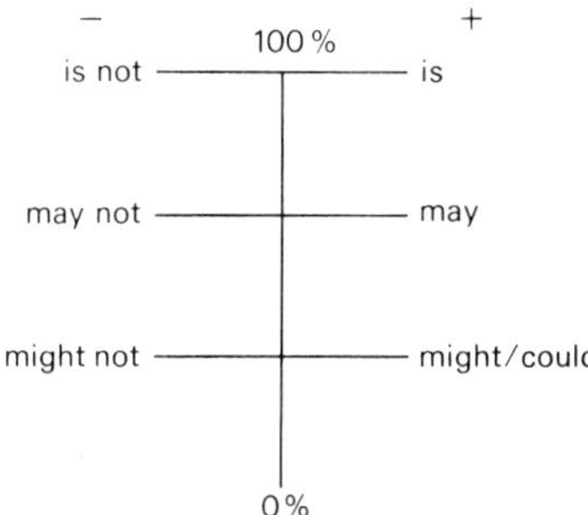

We can also express probability using an adverb or an *it* expression.

EXAMPLES

4. IT IS POSSIBLE THAT this fault is due to a faulty switch.
5. This fault is *possibly* due to a faulty switch.
6. IT IS LIKELY THAT this fault is due to an open circuit.
7. This fault is PROBABLY due to an open circuit.

Note how these expressions fit into the probability scale:

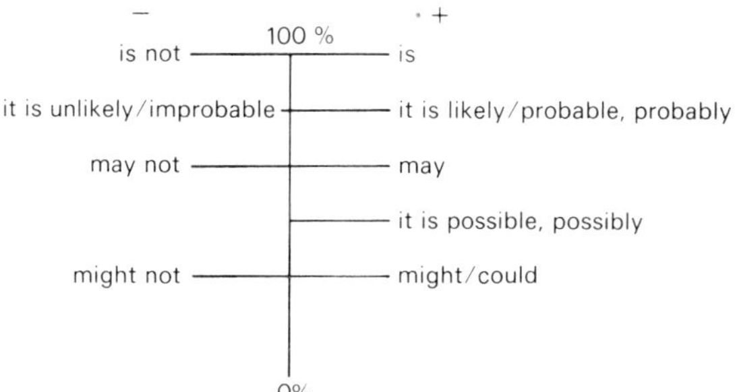

EXERCISE I *Fault finding 5: conclusions*

Now consider the possible results of the tests you suggested in Exercise G:

TEST	RESULT
1. Short-circuit the switch.	The bell rings.
2. Check the supply.	The output is normal.

From these results we can make conclusions.

EXAMPLES

INVESTIGATION	RESULT	CONCLUSION
1. Short-circuit the switch.	The bell rings.	The switch MUST be faulty.
2. Check the supply.	The output is normal.	The supply CANNOT be faulty.

We use *must* or *cannot* for conclusions which we make with complete certainty. Note how we can add them to our probability scale.

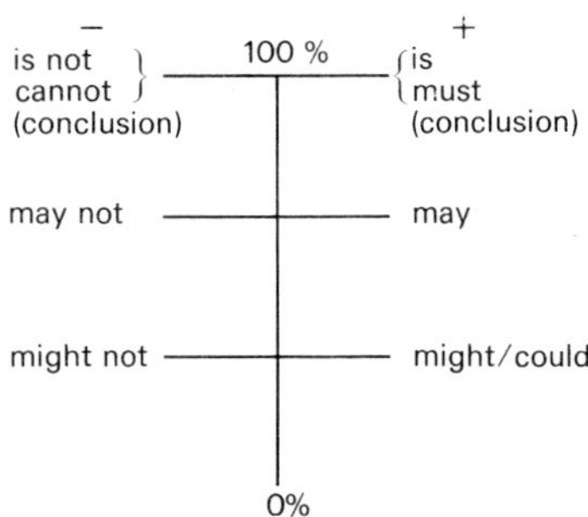

Now study this circuit of a power supply:

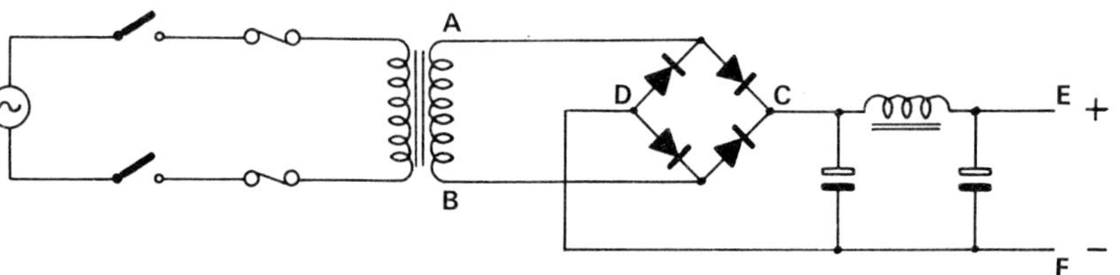

An output meter across EF gives no reading. Study this flow chart which gives a logical method for identifying possible faults. Fill in each of the missing conclusions using *must*. Conclusions 2 and 6 have been given for you.

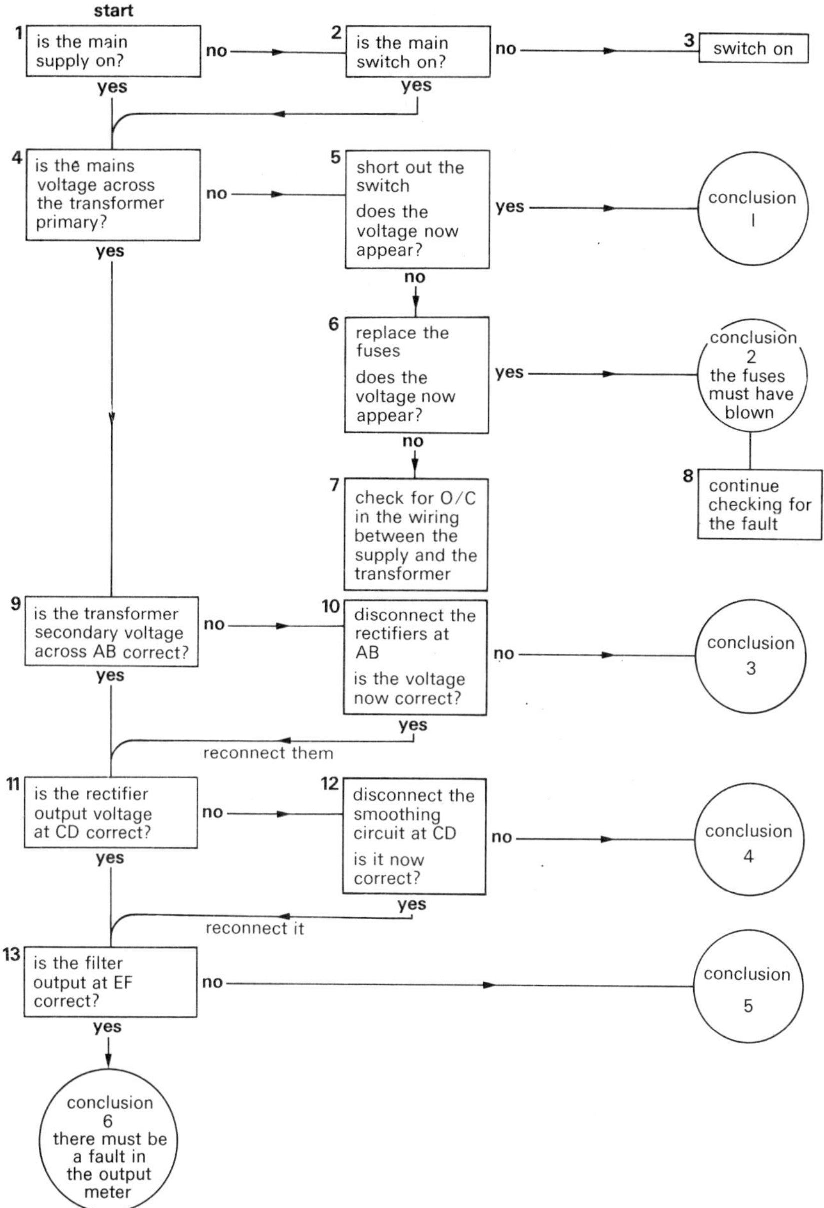
start
1 is the main supply on?
no
yes
2 is the main switch on?
no
yes
3 switch on
4 is the mains voltage across the transformer primary?
no
yes
5 short out the switch
does the voltage now appear?
yes
no
conclusion 1
6 replace the fuses
does the voltage now appear?
yes
no
conclusion 2 the fuses must have blown
7 check for O/C in the wiring between the supply and the transformer
8 continue checking for the fault
9 is the transformer secondary voltage across AB correct?
no
yes
10 disconnect the rectifiers at AB
is the voltage now correct?
no
yes
conclusion 3
reconnect them
11 is the rectifier output voltage at CD correct?
no
yes
12 disconnect the smoothing circuit at CD
is it now correct?
no
yes
conclusion 4
reconnect it
13 is the filter output at EF correct?
no
yes
conclusion 5
conclusion 6 there must be a fault in the output meter

EXERCISE J *Fault finding 6: conclusions*

Make conclusions using *cannot* from each of these results:

1. There is a mains voltage across the transformer input.
2. The transformer secondary voltage across AB is correct.
3. The rectifier output at CD is correct.
4. The filter output at EF is correct.

III INFORMATION TRANSFER

EXERCISE K *Interpreting graphs*

Graphs are produced by linking a number of observations together. Study these observations. They describe the action of a silicon rectifier:

1. When a forward voltage of 1·05 V is applied, a forward current of 3 A flows.
2. When a reverse voltage of 4 V is applied, a reverse current of 3·8 mA flows.

These and other observations are summarized in the two tables below:

Forward characteristics

Current	(A)	3	2·5	2	1·5	1	0·5	0·1
Voltage	(V)	1·05	1	0·9	0·87	0·81	0·75	0·5

Reverse characteristics

Current	(mA)	9	8	6	3·8	2	1·1
Voltage	(V)	9	8	6	4	2	1

Now use the information in the tables to make a graph showing the forward and reverse characteristics of a silicon rectifier. Use the blank graph below:

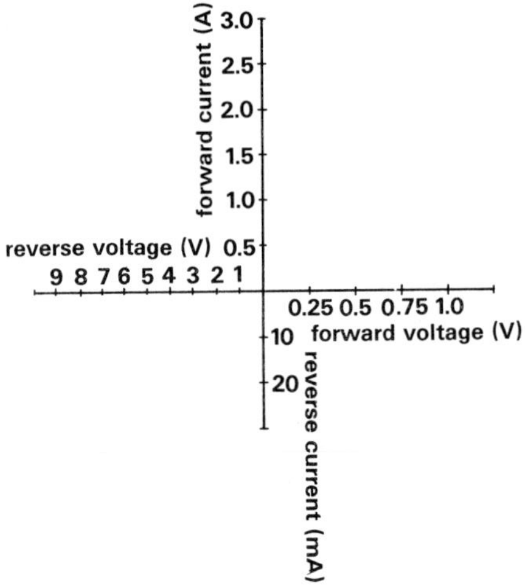

EXERCISE L *Making observations from graphs*

Study this graph. It shows the magnetization curve for a piece of cast steel. The graph has been divided into three important sections:

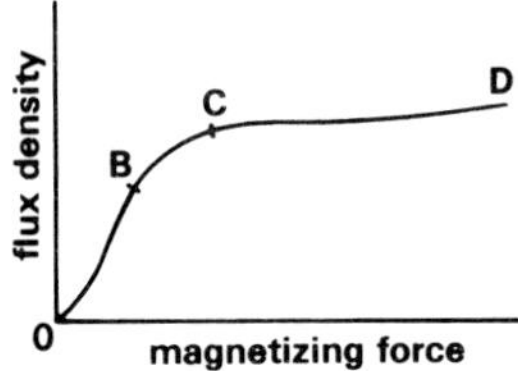

We can make an observation about each section of the graph.

EXAMPLE (section OB)

1. As the magnetizing force increases, the flux density RISES STEEPLY.

We can rewrite this example using an adjective and a noun.

2. As the magnetizing force increases, there is a STEEP RISE in the flux density.

Now make observations for sections BC and CD of the graph.

EXERCISE M *Writing descriptions from graphs*

This graph describes the characteristics of a tunnel diode. Use the information it contains to complete the description below:

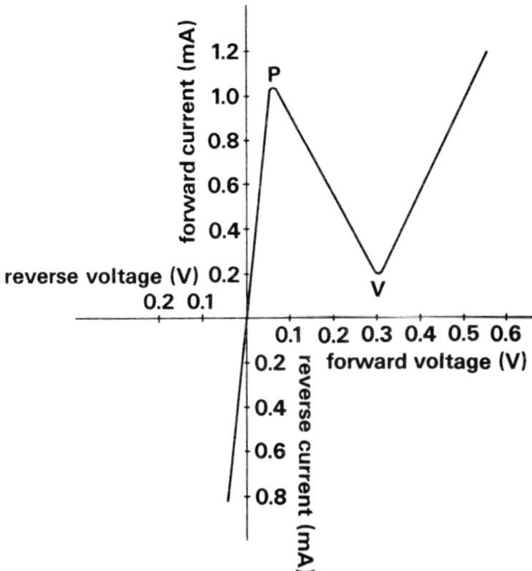

As the forward voltage is increased, the current (1) . . . . . . until point P is reached. P is known as the peak point. The peak voltage for a germanium tunnel diode is about (2) . . . . . . After P the current (3) . . . . . . until V. V is known as the valley point. From P to V the diode has a negative resistance. The forward voltage at V is about (4) . . . . . . After the valley point, the current (5) . . . . . . with increased voltage and the diode behaves like a normal diode. When a reverse voltage is applied however, the reverse current (6) . . . . . . unlike normal diodes.

IV GUIDED WRITING

STAGE 1 *Grouping sentences by topic*

Divide this group of sentences into three paragraphs. The paragraph topics are:

PARAGRAPH 1 How a transformer works
PARAGRAPH 2 The ideal transformer
PARAGRAPH 3 The practical transformer

> The transformer is a device which changes the magnitude of alternating voltages. It consists of two coils, a primary and a secondary, wound round a ferromagnetic core. The coils are insulated from each other. When an alternating voltage is applied to the primary, an emf is induced in the coil. At the same time an emf is induced in the secondary coil. In an ideal transformer the induced emf per turn in the primary coil will equal the emf induced per turn in the secondary. The ideal transformer has no losses in the electric circuit or in the magnetic circuit. In addition, no current is required to magnetize the core and it has losses. These are of three kinds: hysteresis loss, eddy-current loss and winding losses. Hysteresis loss can be reduced by using high-quality steel, eddy-current loss by laminating the core but little can be done about winding losses. In modern transformers they account for a high percentage of the total loss.

STAGE 2 *Adding linking paragraphs*

Linking paragraphs help the reader to find his way through a text. There are three types: introductory, transition and summary.

EXAMPLE: Introductory

> First we shall discuss X and then consider what implications this has for Y. Finally we shall describe Z.

EXAMPLE: Transition

Having discussed X, we must now consider its implications for Y.

Transition paragraphs are usually very short. Often they are reduced to one sentence and are added to the end of one paragraph or the beginning of the following paragraph.

EXAMPLE: Summary

We have shown the importance of X in the development of Y. In addition we have demonstrated the role of Z.

Now add a suitable introductory paragraph, transition paragraphs or sentences and a summary paragraph to the paragraphs in Stage 1.

STAGE 3 *Describing a radio telephone system*

With the aid of this diagram, the notes below and the reading passage on page 93, describe a simple radio telephone system.

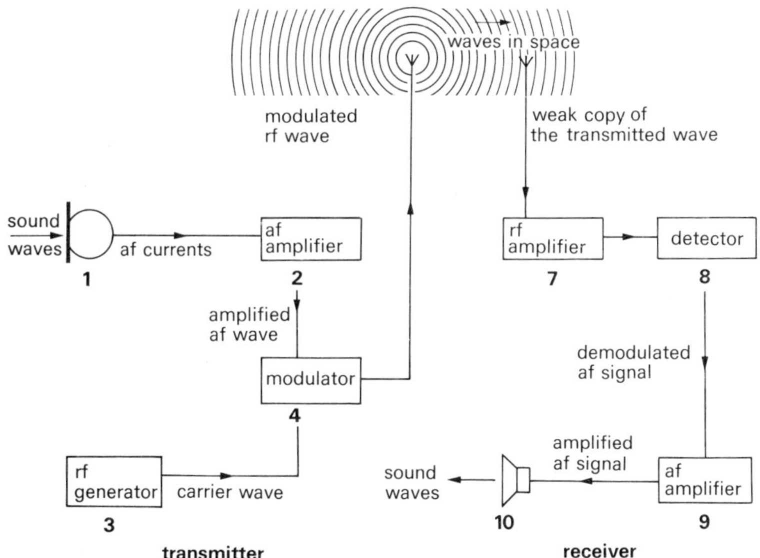

1. microphone: converts sound waves to weak af currents
2. af amplifier: amplifies af currents from the microphone and feeds them to the modulator
3. rf generator: produces a carrier wave of radio frequency
4. modulator: changes the carrier wave according to the amplitude of the af signal from the af amplifier
5. antenna: radiates the modulated rf wave

6. antenna: receives a weak copy of the transmitted modulated rf wave
7. rf amplifier: amplifies the weak rf signal
8. detector: demodulates the rf wave to recover the af signal
9. af amplifier: amplifies the weak af signal
10. loudspeaker: converts the af amplifier output to sound waves which are a copy of those fed into the microphone

V READING AND SUMMARIZING

STAGE 1 *Previewing*

Read the title and lines 1–4. Then write down what you think the passage will be about.

RECTIFYING CIRCUITS

Although mains supplies are normally ac, for many applications a dc supply is required. Where it is uneconomical or impractical to use batteries, the mains ac supply must be converted into dc. We will examine here three rectifying circuits for converting single phase ac supplies into direct current.

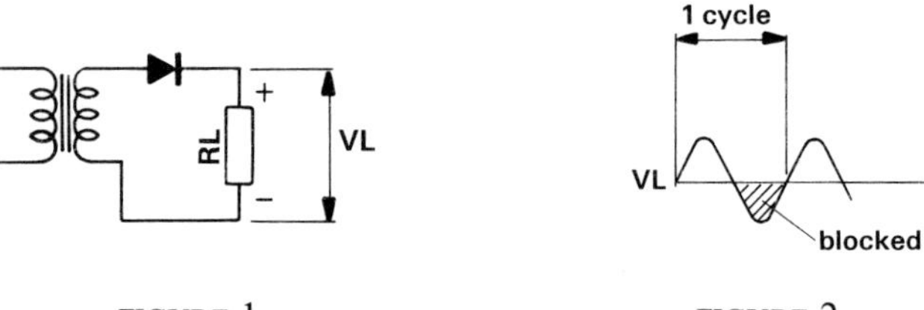

FIGURE 1 FIGURE 2

Figure 1 shows a half-wave rectifier. It incorporates a single diode. The direction of the arrow on the diode symbol indicates the conventional flow of current through the diode. R_L is the resistance of the load and V_L the voltage across the load. An alternating current changes from positive to negative in each cycle. This cycle is repeated 50 or 60 times per second in most ac systems. The resultant waveform is sinusoidal.

Figure 2 shows what happens to the ac sine wave in half wave rectification. In the first half of each cycle, the applied voltage is positive and the diode conducts, allowing current to pass through the load. In the second half, the applied voltage is negative and is blocked by the high resistance of the diode to reverse voltages. This form of rectification has only light current applications. It is not economical in that half the supply waveform is not utilized.

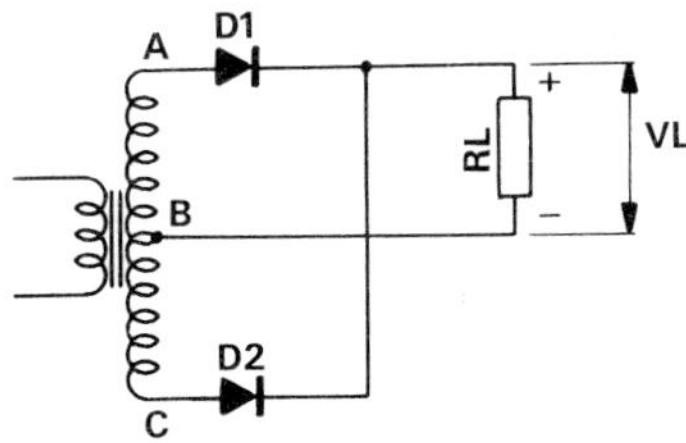

FIGURE 3

The circuit in Figure 3 provides full-wave rectification. It requires a transformer with a centre-tapped secondary and two diodes. The emfs in both halves of the secondary are equal but are of opposite polarity at any instant. Thus when A is positive with respect to B, D1 conducts and the current passes through the load back to B. Similarly when C is positive with respect to B, D2 conducts. Only half the secondary winding time is utilized at any one time.

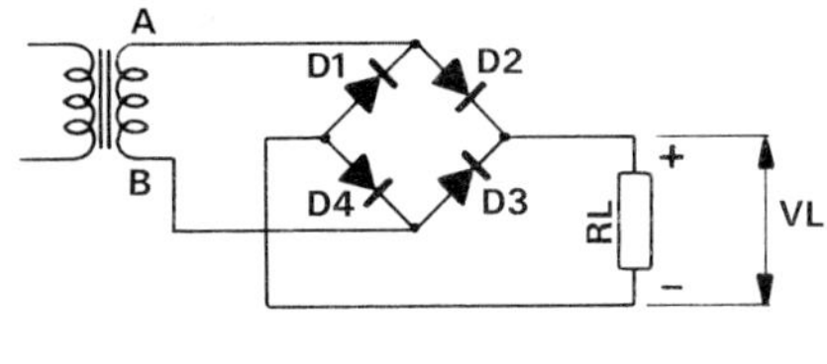

FIGURE 4

The bridge circuit shown in Figure 4 contains four diodes wired as shown to form a bridge. This circuit also provides full-wave rectification but it is more efficient in that all the output of the secondary is utilized. In addition, having four diodes, the peak inverse voltage which any one diode has to withstand is half that of the circuit shown in Figure 3. In the first half of any cycle, A is positive with respect to B and D2 and D4 conduct. D1 and D3 conduct in the second half of the cycle. Bridge circuits have many applications and are to be found in the power supplies of much mains operated electronic equipment. Another common use is in providing low-power dc motor drives.

STAGE 2 *Recognizing rephrasing*

Now read the whole passage carefully. Each of these sentences summarizes part of the passage. Identify the lines summarized:

1. Bridge circuits contain four diodes; two conduct in the positive half and two conduct in the negative half of each cycle. (lines . . . . . .)
2. The passage describes three methods of rectifying single-phase ac supplies. (lines . . . . . .)
3. One method of full-wave rectification uses a centre-tapped secondary and two diodes. (lines . . . . . .)
4. Bridge circuits are preferred because they utilize all the transformer output and the diodes have to withstand lower inverse voltages. (lines . . . . . .)
5. The centre-tapped transformer provides two equal outputs which are opposite in polarity, thus one diode is conducting at any instant. (lines . . . . . .)
6. Half-wave circuits use a single diode to pass the positive half of each cycle but block the negative half. (lines . . . . . .)

STAGE 3 *Summarizing*

Put the sentences in Stage 2 in the correct order and use them to make a paragraph summarizing the passage. You may add words of your own to make a good paragraph. Make sure no information is repeated unnecessarily.

Appendices

I MATHEMATICAL SYMBOLS USED IN ELECTRICAL ENGINEERING AND ELECTRONICS

SYMBOL	EXAMPLE	MEANING IN FULL
$\cdot$	$3{\cdot}14159$	three *point* one four one five nine
$+$	$R_1 + R_2$	R one *plus* R two
$-$	$V - V_1$	V *minus* V one
$\pm$	$\pm$ 3 dB	*plus or minus* three decibels
$=$	$R = R_1 + R_2$	R *equals/is equal to* R one plus R two
$\approx$ or $\triangleq$	$I \approx 28$ mA	I *is approximately equal to* twenty eight milliamps
$\times$	$f \times 120$	f *times/multiplied by* one hundred and twenty
no sign between two quantities	$E = IR$	E equals I *times/multiplied by* R
one quantity over another	$\frac{I}{R}$	I *over/divided by* R *The ratio of* I *to* R
$\propto$	$I \propto V$	I *is proportional* to V
$:$	$11:1$	eleven *to* one
$\%$	10%	ten *per cent*
$^\circ$	30°C	thirty *degrees* celcius (Centigrade)
$\sqrt{}$	$\sqrt{5}$	*the square root of/root of* five
^{2} ^{3}	R^2 X^3	R *squared*; X *cubed*
$^{-8}$	10^4 10^{-8}	ten *to the power four*; ten *to the power minus eight*
$>$	>10dB	*greater than* ten decibels
$<$	<25mA	*less than* twenty-five milliamps
$\leqslant$	$\leqslant 5$W	*less than or equal to* five watts

II TERMS, SYMBOLS, UNITS AND ABBREVIATIONS USED IN ELECTRICAL ENGINEERING AND ELECTRONICS

TERM	SYMBOL	UNIT	ABBREVIATION
admittance	Y	siemens	S
capacitance	C	farad	F
charge	Q	coulomb	C
conductance	G	siemens	S
conductivity	σ (sigma) γ (gamma)	siemens per metre	S/m
current	I	ampere	A
electric field strength	E	volt per metre	V/m
electric flux	Q	coulomb	C
electric flux density	D	coulomb per square metre	C/m^2
electromotive force	E	volt	V
frequency	f	hertz	Hz
frequency, angular	ω (omega)	radian per second	rad/s
frequency, resonant	fr	hertz	Hz
gain	A	—	—
inductance	L	henry	H
inductance, mutual	M	henry	H
impedance	Z	ohm	Ω
magnetic field strength	H	ampere per metre	A/m
magnetic flux	ϕ (phi)	weber	Wb
magnetic flux density	B	tesla	T
magnetomotive force	F	ampere	A
permeability	μ (mu)	henry per metre	H/m
permittivity	ε (epsilon)	farad per metre	F/m
phase angle	ϕ (phi)	radian	rad
power, apparent	S	volt-ampere	VA
power, reactive	Q	var	vars
power, true	P	watt	W

reactance	X	ohm	Ω
reactance, capacitive	X_C	ohm	Ω
reactance, inductive	X_L	ohm	Ω
reluctance	S	ampere per weber	A/Wb
resistance	R	ohm	Ω
resistivity	ρ (rho)	ohm per metre	Ω/m
susceptance	B	siemens	S
voltage	V	volt	V

III CIRCUIT SYMBOLS USED IN THIS BOOK

1. resistor 
2. variable resistor 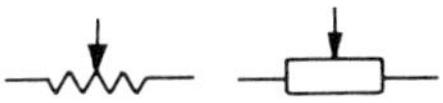
3. capacitor 
4. variable capacitor 
5. electrolytic capacitor 
6. coil/winding 
7. choke/iron-cored inductor 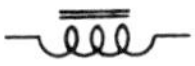
8. transformer 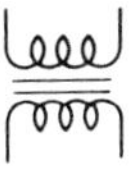
9. switch 
10. fuse
11. cell 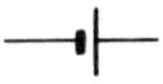
12. microphone 
13. loudspeaker 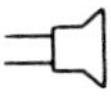
14. bulb/lamp 
15. diode 
16. Zener diode 
17. pnp transistor 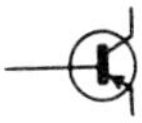
18. npn transistor 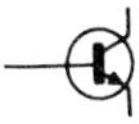
19. milliammeter 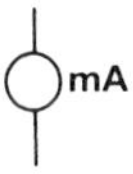 mA
20. voltmeter  V
21. motor  M
22. bell
23. antenna 
24. earth/ground